Revelation
unwrapped

Revelation
unwrapped

JOHN RICHARDSON

MPA Books - Biblical Application Series
Revelation Unwrapped
John P. Richardson

Published in the United Kingdom by St
Matthias Press/MPA Books

Distributed exclusively in the UK by:
St Matthias Press
PO Box 665
London SW20 8RL
Tel: 0181 947 5686
Fax: 0181 944 7091
E-mail: 100332.2225@compuserve.com

ISBN 0 9524894 2 2 (UK)

Published in Australia by
Mathews Park Avenue Books,
9, Cudgee Close, Baulkham Hills, NSW 2153

ISBN 0 646 28287 5 (AUS)

Designed by Kevin Wade

Contents

Preface

▦ A BOOK OF BLESSING

The book of the Revelation to John certainly generates more anxiety amongst Christians than any other book in the Bible. A 'Happy Hunting Ground' for cults and sects like Jehovah's Witnesses, it is often the 'Slough of Despond' for the orthodox believer. This is a great shame, because (as the title suggests) it is supposed to *reveal* things to us, and its opening verses say God caused the book to be written so we may be blessed by acting on what it says: "Blessed is he who reads aloud the words of the prophecy, and blessed are those who hear, and who keep what is written therein..." (1:3).

The main reason why Revelation doesn't bless us, however, is because we are put off reading it! And this is largely due to the form in which it is written. Revelation fits into the literary category known as 'Apocalyptic' – a style of writing, familiar in the first century AD, with its own conventions of symbols and visions. However, because this style is not so familiar to us, we miss the *blessing* because we miss the *message*. In this book we will be trying first and foremost to understand Revelation in the way that John would have expected his first-century readers to understand it. In general this means understanding Revelation within the total Biblical context.

▦ TRUTH AND SCHOLARSHIP

During the series of Bible studies which originally led to the writing of this book, one girl (actually a member of a well-known cult) objected that I'd offered a number of opinions on the meaning of particular passages. She didn't want 'opinions', she just wanted 'the truth'! So perhaps I should make it clear where I stand on discovering the truth about what the Bible teaches.

In 2 Timothy 2:7 Paul wrote "Think over what I say, for the Lord will grant you understanding in everything." Dick Lucas, a leading English evangelical, helpfully emphasizes the combination here of our thought and the Lord's help in reaching a true understanding of the Bible. As an evangelical who is not a liberal I believe there is one truth. However, I also believe that, until we are sure what that truth is, Christians may properly differ in their opinions. Furthermore, as an evangelical who is not a fundamentalist, I agree that human reason is essential to reaching that truth. Finally, as an evangelical who is not a post-modernist, I believe that the truth of a text lies ultimately in the meaning of the author – which in the case of Scripture includes both the human and the divine 'authors'. I am aware of the questions raised by the study of hermeneutics, but I simply note that even the most ardent enthusiasts of post-modernism still express their opinions in books. (Let the reader understand – and those who don't needn't worry about it!)

Some readers may feel I have given too much weight to the opinions of 'scholars' (though others will recognize I mention far too few). Scholars don't hold all the answers, but scholarship helps determine the extent to which opinions should be heeded. Evangelical scholarship accepts the authority of the Bible and the work of the Holy Spirit in the believer. However, it also recognizes that since God has chosen to reveal himself through particular words in a particular context, we need to use our reasoning skills to understand what has been revealed. A scholar is simply someone familiar with the relevant material (including the multitude of books and articles, and the opinions of others concerning the subject in hand) who has properly weighed the evidence and demonstrates the plausibility of his or her conclusions.

The commentary I would most recommend for those who want to read further is *I Saw Heaven Opened*, by Michael Wilcock (London: Inter-Varsity Press, 1975), now published as *The Message of Revelation* in the 'Bible Speaks Today' series. This provided the basis for the studies which led to this book. The other main references (in author's alphabetical order) were as follows:

The Revelation of St John the Divine
G B Caird (London: A & C Black, 1966)

The Gospel in Revelation
G Goldsworthy (Carlisle: The Paternoster Press, 1994)
More than Conquerors
W Hendriksen (Grand Rapids: Baker Book House, 1990)
The Book of Revelation
P E Hughes (Leicester: Inter-Varsity Press, 1990)

Other books and articles have been noted in the text. The greatest aid to reading Revelation, however, is a good concordance and in preparing this book I have found my computer-based concordance invaluable.

John Richardson
Anglican Chaplain to the University of East London
September 1996

Chapter 1

The background to the Book

■ DATE AND AUTHORSHIP

Following early tradition, commentators have tended to date the writing of Revelation around 90AD. However, there are reasons (also compatible with tradition) for believing it could have been written earlier than 70AD. J A T Robinson, in particular, argues for this view in *Redating the New Testament* (London: SCM, 1976). The writer names himself as "John" (1:9) and tradition also identifies him with the Apostle and the writer of the Gospel and Epistles bearing his name. D Guthrie's *New Testament Introduction* (London: IVP, 1970) gives a thorough review of the arguments about authorship and dating. Guthrie comments that though the arguments in favour of John's authorship are inconclusive, "At least, if this is the true solution it at once explains the rise of the tradition, which none of the others satisfactorily does" (p 949). As this conclusion is congruous with the content of Revelation, we will be assuming throughout that it was set down by the Apostle John and that it was, as he says, initially revealed to him by Jesus. The exact nature of his *experience* must necessarily remain a mystery. However, our ignorance at this point need not prevent us understanding the message of the book.

■ REVELATION AND HISTORY

One of the main problems with studying Revelation is its relationship with history. Throughout this book we will use a 'time-line' to indicate how each section we are studying is being related to human history, even though we will not always tie this to particular events. The key points on this time-line are:

BC	=	Before Christ
AD	=	*Anno Domini*, the time after Christ's birth.

THE FUTURE	=	The period (of unknown length) from now to the second coming.
THE AGE TO COME	=	The period subsequent to Christ's Second Coming.
†	=	The death, resurrection and ascension of Jesus.
REV	=	The time at which John received Revelation (between 70 and 90AD).
▲	=	The present.
AX	=	The time of the Antichrist
SC	=	The second coming of Jesus.

Our basic 'time line' looks like this (the relative periods are not to scale):

Over it, we will fit the various parts of the book as we proceed. Thus, chapters 2 and 3 fit as follows:

If we cannot be sure where a particular passage 'fits', this is indicated with a question mark, e.g.: 9:1-21?

Our overall understanding of the relationship of Revelation with history directly affects its interpretation. Is it a book which *had* a message once, or perhaps a book which *will have* a message to a generation of Christians in the future? Or has it a message for *every* Christian in *every* age? In this respect, there are four 'schools of interpretation' which can be summarized as follows:

Preterist – Revelation describes PAST events written as if it were 'prophecy'. This is the view of many liberal scholars. It allows the book to have a message for us today – but not a predictive message for the future.

Historicist – Revelation describes the WHOLE OF HISTORY, particularly from 70AD to the return of Christ. This was the view of many Reformation scholars. It allows the book to have both a message for today and an element of prediction.

Futurist – Revelation deals principally with events of the FUTURE 'END TIMES'. This is the view of many modern popular writers, especially in America. This means whilst the book is interesting to read now, it will only be *practically* relevant at some time in the future.

Idealist – Revelation is entirely symbolic and DOES NOT REFER TO ANY SPECIFIC EVENTS at all. Again, it allows the book to be relevant today, though the meaning may not be immediately obvious.

We can relate each of these views to our 'time line' as follows:

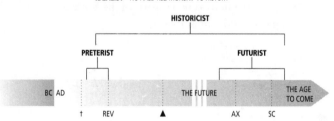

There are problems with all these views. However, the position we will be taking is basically a mixture of 'Historicist' and 'Idealist'.

■ REVELATION AND SCRIPTURE

Most of the imagery in Revelation is drawn from other books in the Bible. It is therefore important in reading Revelation to realize that *it is not usually adding new information so much as summarizing old.* Many of these allusions to other parts of Scripture will be noted as we go along. Frequently they are single verses, but these should not be seen as isolated 'proof texts' so much as *examples* of the background material to a particular passage or concept. Obviously it has been impossible to note all of these allusions, or even always to be aware of them! At some stage you should get hold of a Bible with footnoted references and see the wealth of material John draws on.

You will get the most benefit out of this book if you actually read the cross-references given in the text. The following conventions have been used for those Bible references:

• Chapters and verses are indicated by "Shortened-book-name N:n". Thus "Gen 3:15" means "the book of Genesis, chapter 3, verse 15". (There is a list of abbreviations in Appendix B.)
• Gen 3:15a means the first part of Gen 3:15, 3:15b means the part after 15a, and so on.
• All verse numbers are *inclusive*.
• cf means "compare with" (i.e. look these verses up!).
• All emphases in Scripture quotations have been added for the purposes of this book.

▓ THE STRUCTURE OF REVELATION

It is clear to any reader that Revelation has a definite structure, but precise analyses of this vary. Most commentators divide the book into seven main sections – with or without a Prologue or Epilogue. The following structure is used in this book:

Introduction
Prologue (1:1-20)
The Letters to the Seven Churches (2:1-3:22)

Main Section
The Seven Seals (4:1-8:1)
The Seven Trumpets (8:2-11:18)
The Holy War (11:19-15:4)
The Seven Plagues (15:5-16:21)
The Fall of Babylon (17:1-19:10)
The Conquering King (19:11-21)
The Reigning Saints (20:1-21:8)

The Final Act
The New Jerusalem (21:9-22:5)
Final Instructions and Exhortations (22:6-21)

Exercises (Throughout this book you will find exercises and questions as you go along. You don't have to tackle these, but obviously they are designed to help your understanding. You may find the questions useful for group discussion.)

• Read through Revelation in one sitting and note in your Bible the sections given above.
• See whether you would like to make additional or different sub-divisions.

Chapter 2

Introduction
Revelation1:1-3:22

■ 1:1-20 PROLOGUE

Greetings and Outline of the Message 1:1-8

This part of the book of Revelation is relatively easy to locate historically since it belongs to the point in time at which John received the vision. We are told by v.9 that he was on the island of Patmos, off the coast of Greece, apparently in exile "on account of the word of God and the testimony of Jesus" (1:9, a phrase that will recur throughout the book). Notice there is an impressive 'chain of authority' to Revelation. It is revealed by the Father (1:1, here we take "God" to mean "God the Father", cf 1 Pet 1:2, etc.), to the Son, via an angel, through John (1:2), in the Spirit (1:10), for Christians. We should therefore be ready to listen to what it says!

Strictly speaking, the book has three 'Introductions'. John introduces the book in 1:1-3. He introduces himself to "the seven churches" with greetings from God (the Father, Sevenfold Spirit and Son) in 1:4-5. And in 1:9-11 he introduces the visions he received. Notice that vv. 4-6 read rather like the standard beginning of an epistle (cf Gal 1:3-4; 1 Pet 1:1-2), which indicates that the book truly belongs in the mainstream of New Testament literature.

The mention of the "seven spirits" in 1:4 may be a clue to understanding the book. John's audience were probably as surprised as we are to see this phrase. However, we know from 22:17 that the Apostle believed in one Holy Spirit (not seven): "The Spirit and the Bride say, 'Come.'" The effect of this phrase is to alert us to the number seven – which is mentioned fifty-four times in Revelation. On investigation, we find that the book follows repeated patterns of sevens (see our suggested structure above), and within the subdivisions of the book there are often seven smaller sections. The number seven indeed seems to be a key to help us unlock the structure of the book.

These introductory verses also show that the focus of Revelation will be on the *gospel* (1:5b-6, cf Ex 19:6), on *Christ's return and the accompanying judgement* (1:7, cf Dan 7:13 and Zech 12:10), and on *God as the Lord of history* (1:8). God's description of himself as the "Alpha and the Omega" (1:8) refers to the first and last letters of the Greek alphabet and means he is *before* all things and *beyond* all time. This last point is crucial to our understanding of the message of Revelation since it prevents us insisting that the sequence of the book simply follows the 'linear' pattern of human time.

NUMBER SYMBOLISM IN REVELATION

The fact that in Revelation certain numbers (e.g. three, seven, twelve, etc.) appear frequently, and others (e.g. eight, nine or eleven) not at all, suggests to us that these numbers are symbolic. (It would be unusual, even in the providence of God, if every-thing that needed to be numbered occurred only in such a limited range!) Numbers in Revelation are *qualitative* rather than *quantitative*. That is to say, they tell us about the *nature* of things rather than their *amount*. In English we often use a 'dozen' in this way, as in "I've told you *dozens* of times". This doesn't mean "The number of times I've told you divides exactly by twelve" but "I've told you often enough". The commonest numbers and their likely symbolism in Revelation are as follows:

3 – Hebrew uses repetition for emphasis - "Holy, holy, holy" = "the most holy".

3½ – half of 7 (see below).

4 – the whole of creation (e.g. the "four corners of the earth").

6 – 1 short of 7.

7 – the complete or perfect number, or the essence of things ("I have sailed the seven seas").

10 – a number of magnitude ("many" or "many times" – in English we tend to use "a dozen").

12 – the number of God's people – Israel (tribes) or the church (apostles).

24 – 12 *plus* 12 – the people of God under the Old and New Covenants.

42 – the number of months in 3½ years of 12 months each.

144 – 12 *times* 12 – the total number of the whole people of God.

666 – work it out! (7 minus 1, 3 times)

1,000 – 10 cubed (multi-plied by itself 3 times) – the 'most superlative' number (cf 10 and 3).

1,260 – the number of days in 3½ years of twelve 30-day months.

The Start of the Visions: The Lord of the Churches 1:9-20

John's personal context (which he shares with his initial readers) sets the pattern for the whole book. It is one of "tribulation and the kingdom and the patient endurance ... on account of the word of God and the testimony of Jesus" (1:9). John's vision, however, is about to lift him out of these surroundings! "In the Spirit on the Lord's day" (1:10), he hears a voice behind him announcing a message for "the seven churches" (1:11) which he is to write down and send to them.

In an earlier passage about God's comfort in suffering, Isaiah had promised "a word behind you" to guide his people (Isa 30:21) and a "Teacher" who would be seen (Isa 30:20). For John, and for us, the word here precedes sight, but turning to see who is speaking, he sees first "seven golden lampstands" (1:12). For someone familiar with the Old Testament, these lampstands would immediately suggest the Tabernacle in the wilderness (Ex 25:31-40), and therefore the presence of God. But then amongst the lampstands John sees "one like a son of man" (1:13). This term was Jesus' own favourite description of himself (e.g. Mk 14:62, etc.), and the subsequent description of this figure (particularly 1:18, "I died, and behold I am alive for evermore") tells us that John is indeed seeing Jesus in his vision. However, a comparison of his description (1:13-16) with the "Ancient of Days" in Daniel 7:9-10 (who is God himself, before whom "one like a son of man" appears, Dan 7:13) reminds us that Jesus is 'as one' with the Father (cf John 10:30). John is seeing the Jesus who is like a son of man, but now in all his Divine Glory.

This Jesus tells John again to write down what he is about to see (1:19). But he also gives him (and us) a further key to interpret what he will see, by explaining the "mystery" (1:20) of the seven stars and lampstands. In the New Testament, a 'mystery' is actually something known – but only because it is revealed by God (cf Eph 3:4-5). The 'mysterious' objects here – stars and lampstands – stand for less mysterious realities, namely angels and churches (see below on angels). Thus what John is seeing is a vision of the Lord of the church in the midst of the churches and controlling their spiritual destiny. It is a vision of the heavenly 'control room' and of the one who is in control of us and our future. Though in the rest of Revelation it may not always be clear exactly what is being symbolized, 1:20 makes the important point that the things which

John *sees* in his vision *can be related to things we can identify in our theology or our experience.*

"THE ANGEL OF THE CHURCH..."

There are a number of opinions as to what might be meant by "the angel" of each church. Some have suggested it means the church leader. Others, on the grounds that the word simply means "a messenger", have suggested it refers to the person who took the original copy of the book of Revelation to each church. On balance, however, especially given the way John refers to angels in the rest of Revelation, it probably refers to a spiritual being. We needn't understand from this that each congregation has a 'guardian angel', but rather we are reminded that the life of each earthly church involves an intimate connection with heavenly realities (cf 1 Cor 11:10; Heb 12:22).

- Why does a book addressed to suffering Christians start with a vision of heaven?
- At this stage, what would you say is the main purpose of the Book of Revelation?

◼ THE LETTERS TO THE SEVEN CHURCHES 2:1-3:22

John descends immediately in his vision from the heavenly 'control room' to hear a description of the earthly church. The situations in "the seven churches" were real situations which his readers would have recognized. The letters themselves are relatively easy to understand, and for that reason we will not spend long on them in this book. However, there is more here than first meets the eye. In particular, *there is a formal structure to the section.* Each letter follows a very similar pattern. Also the longest is in the middle, and letters two and six contain no condemnation(see the diagram below).

This structure suggests these letters are not just a random

LETTER 1	LETTER 2	LETTER 3	LETTER 4	LETTER 5	LETTER 6	LETTER 7
A fault	No faults	Some faults	Major faults	Some faults	No faults	Major faults
Promise: To eat from the tree of life	Promise: Not hurt by the second death	Promise: The hidden manna, a white stone and a new name	Promise: Power over the nations to rule them and the morning star	Promise: White garments, name kept in the book of life and before God	Promise: to be a pillar in the temple and the names of God, the new city and Christ	Promise: To sit on Christ's throne

collection. There were at least ten towns with churches in this province of Asia at this time, so these seven churches were probably picked to be *representative* of the church in that place and time – and therefore, to an extent, in every place and time. For this reason, we may reject the idea that they represent the church in *successive* ages (unless we can show that the history of the church follows such a neat symmetry).

The letters present to us a serious picture of church life – not of vicarage tea parties, nor of 'praise concerts', but of a situation where matters of life and death are at stake, and where constant vigilance is called for. Perhaps most surprisingly, we see that the *Lord of the church* can also be the *Judge of the churches*. However, the individual believer need never lose heart. In every church, even one as bad as that at Laodicea, there is always a promise to the one "who conquers" (3:21).

- Look up the articles on the towns where these churches were in a Bible dictionary and see how their features relate to each letter.
- Note some of the problems these churches encountered. See if you can relate them to your own situation.
- The promises in this section of Revelation (e.g. the "tree of life", the "second death", the "new name") recur throughout the book. Note these down as you come across them.

The churches mentioned have clearly faced some mistreatment (2:3,9; 3:8), yet it does not appear to have been particularly severe. Their members have rarely been threatened with imprisonment or death (2:10). Indeed, persecution seems to lie in the future and martyrs seem to be so few they are known by name (2:13). Most of the problems addressed seem to be internal rather than external, and there is far more criticism of the churches than of the societies in which they are set. The emphasis appears to be much more on purifying the churches to face future hardships than on encouraging them in present difficulties. All this might suggest an early date for Revelation.

A number of problems are highlighted by these letters, using Old Testament characters (Balaam, Jezebel) as archetypes. Even at this early stage, heretical groups ("the Nicolaitans" 2:6,15) and individuals ("the woman" 2:20) have emerged. Life in the New Testament church was just as big a mess as it is in the present, which should both encourage and warn us. A "lampstand" can be removed from its place (2:5). Though the church has continued in every generation, and is still alive today, the congregations in the areas named here (now modern Turkey) have virtually disappeared.

- What action would you take in your local church on the basis of the advice given here in Revelation?
- What sort of lessons should we be learning from the seven churches?
- What solutions does Jesus propose for the problems in each church?
- What does he call for from individuals?
- What is the purpose of God in allowing the persecution of his people? (2:10, cf Zech 13:8-9)

Summary

In the opening part of his vision, John is shown the church 'warts and all'. This is the church which is going to have to survive "what must soon take place" (1:1), and it is this church which has survived in every generation. However, John could have been forgiven for asking how this would be possible – and the next part of his vision begins to give the answer

Chapter 3

Main Section

Revelation 4:1-21:8

■ THE SEVEN SEALS 4:1-8:1

The Heavenly Throne Room 4:1-11

4:1 – 5:15 stand 'outside time'

For the first time, but not the last, John now sees an opening in heaven – this time "an open door" (4:1, cf 19:11). There are many parallels in what follows with the visions of Isaiah (Isa 6:1-4) and Ezekiel (Ezek 1). However, it is important to ask ourselves how John's vision adapts these parallels, and how they relate to the overall message of the book.

One great theme of the Bible is that God is King and will establish his Kingdom on earth (cf 1 Sam 8:4-7, Psa 2, Mk 1:14). So here, the vision of "one seated on the throne" focuses on *God as King*. At the same time, he is accompanied by symbols which tell us he is the God of the Old Covenant. The precious stones (4:3) remind us of his creativity expressed in Eden (cf Ezek 28:13) and also his Covenant with Israel (Ex 28:17-21). The rainbow (4:3) reminds us of his Covenant with creation (Gen 9:12). The lightning, voices and peals of thunder (4:5) remind us of his appearance at Sinai where the Law was given (Ex 20:18). The crystal 'sea of glass' (4:6) reminds us of the setting for the Covenant meal eaten by Moses and the Israelite elders in the presence of God on Mt Sinai (Ex 24:9-11). The central message, however, is that *this God rules*, and it will be fundamentally important to John and his readers as the more unnerving aspects of his vision are revealed.

The 'kingship', or rule, of God is, however, something which he graciously shares with his human creatures (cf Gen 1:26; Psa 8:3-8). Thus John also sees twenty-four other thrones with twenty-four "elders" seated on them (4:4). The number is clearly symbolic (see above), and the later reference to the names of the twelve tribes of Israel on the gates of the New Jerusalem (21:12) and of the twelve apostles on its foundations (21:14) suggests that twenty-four represents here the people of God under the Old and New Covenants. Ephesians 2:6 says that we are *already* seated with Christ in heaven, so that we have here a symbol of the *whole* church as it is eternally – ascended and ruling with Christ.

Between the elders and the throne John sees also the Spirit of God (4:5) symbolized by "seven torches" (or "lamps", cf Matt 25:1). Earlier, the lampstands reminiscent of the Tabernacle were seen as symbols of the churches throughout the world (1:12, 20). The *lamps* in the Tabernacle, however, were separate from the *lampstands* (Ex 25:37) And in a rather complex image in Zechariah 4, the oil of the lamps is connected with the work of the Spirit (Zech 4:2-3, 6, 12-14). So we may see the Spirit here in Revelation as the *active ingredient* in the life of each of these churches (cf Acts 2:3). We need to remind ourselves, however, that John no more thought the Holy Spirit was 'really' seven lamps than he thought that God was 'really' someone sitting on a throne – or that the church was 'really' only twenty-four people! The "seven spirits" (or "sevenfold Spirit", NIV) *symbolize* the ONE Holy Spirit in his perfection or essence (see above on number symbolism).

Then John sees, *between* the elders and the throne, four fantastic creatures (4:6-8). Their appearance is clearly like that of the cherubim (angelic beings) seen by Ezekiel bearing God's throne (Ezek 10:15, cf Ezek 1). But the appearance of these creatures (4:7) links them to the creation we inhabit, and a clue to their *significance* is found in 1 Ki 7:29 where a similar combination of lions, oxen and cherubim occurs in the Temple decorations. This tells us that we are in the 'Temple presence' of God (cf Isa 6:1). However, we must remember that "temple" and "palace" are the same word in Hebrew and the Temple is thus first and foremost *the place from which God rules the world*. Moreover, the symbols of animals and plants in the *original* Temple also suggest to us that the Temple was a reminder of the garden of Eden, where God's creation was perfectly expressed and his Kingdom was perfectly present[1]. Furthermore, in Isa 11:6-7 we find a bringing together of man (a child), the lion, the ox and other creatures when God's new creation is brought in. Thus, the creatures here also represent *the perfect, restored creation in the presence of the Creator*. The action of "bowing down" (4:10, translated as "worship") is the acknowledgement of God's reign. The creatures (restored creation) and the elders (the reigning church) are encouraging one another in praising and paying homage to God (4:8-11). As the creatures sing God's praises, the elders cast down their crowns in recognition that their reign comes from God, the Sovereign Lord of All.

The Sealed Scroll 5:1-5

At this point, however, John becomes aware of an unusual scroll "written within and on the back" in the right hand of the figure on the throne (5:1). Writing on both sides of a scroll indicated having a great deal to say. ("Written on the back as well, and even so not yet finished", wrote the satirist Juvenal of an overlong poem.) A similar scroll was also seen by Ezekiel (Ezek 2:9-10) and in his vision "there were written on it *words of lamentation and mourning and woe*". This should guide us in understanding what was written on the scroll John saw, especially since there is a similarity to the "flying scroll" in Zech 5:1-3, which was "the curse that goes out over the face of the whole land". The scroll John sees is also unusual in being sealed with *seven* seals which cannot be opened (5:3). In the context of Old Testament prophecy, 'seals' related to matters belonging to the end-times and to judgement (e.g. Deut 32:34-35). Sealing also referred to things whose meaning would only be revealed in the future (e.g. Isa 29:11; Dan 12:4,9, but cf Rev 22:10). Putting all these elements together, we have here *prophetic words of coming judgement on human sin which no-one in earth or heaven could deal with*.

We must appreciate the significance of the sealed scroll to understand the message of the Bible as a whole. In the very presence of God, this scroll, representing the problem of human sin, is an unresolved difficulty because "no-one was found *worthy*" to open it (5:4). Even in his vision, John is deeply distressed, for it introduces a tension to which there seems to be no resolution.

1. See W J Dumbrell *The End of the Beginning: Revelation 21-22 and the Old Testament* (Homebush West: Lancer Books, 1985) p 52.

Then, John hears from one of the elders the answer to the problem (5:5). There is one who is worthy – "the Lion of the tribe of Judah", though this is an ambivalent title signifying both power and judgement (cf Gen 49:9; Hos 5:14-15). However, taken together with the title "the Root of David" (cf Isa 11:10), it identifies the 'worthy one' as being the Messiah.

The Slain Lamb 5:6-10

John hears the announcement of "the Lion of Judah". However, he next sees, "a Lamb standing, as though it had been slain" (5:6). This paradox of 'strength in weakness' is the paradox of God's solution to the problem of human sin (cf 1 Cor 1:18). The Lamb is a symbol of sacrifice (cf Gen 22:7; Isa 53:7, etc.). He is thus the Redeemer, but redemption always carries with it an element of judgement.

The Lamb is described as standing literally "in the midst of the throne and the four living creatures and in the midst of the elders" (5:6). Rather than meaning he is in two places at once (!), this probably means "at the throne, surrounded by the creatures and the elders" (but cf RSV). The description of the Lamb further underlines his nature. The number seven speaks of that which is complete or perfect. Thus his seven horns (5:6) indicate complete power (cf 1 Sam 2:1). His seven eyes are here revealed specifically as the "seven spirits" (or perfect Spirit) of God which proceed from God and the Lamb into the world (cf Zech 4:10). However, eyes are also associated with knowledge (cf Jer 23:24) and here the Lamb's knowledge is depicted as perfect.

Thus the Lamb, who in his human nature is a relation of David (5:5, cf Rom 1:3), has the power, the Spirit and the omniscience of God and is thus able to open the scroll. When he takes the scroll there is therefore a fresh outburst of homage from the four creatures and the elders, accompanied now by harps, incense (which is here specified as the prayers of God's people, 5:8) and "a new song" (5:9a). Significantly, in the Old Testament, "new songs" were always sung to Yahweh, the Lord himself (cf Psa 96:1 etc.). Thus the singing of a "new song" to the Lamb signifies his divine nature. The content of the song (5:9b-10) is a summary of the gospel (cf Rev 1:5-6; Ex 19:5-6; 1 Pet 2:9). The solution to the problem of sin is found in the Lamb and his death as Divine Sin-bearer.

The Growing Circle 5:11-14

Added to the circle around the throne, John then sees millions of angels who join in praising God with the four living creatures and the elders (5:11-12, cf Heb 12:22-24). They also praise "the Lamb who was slain". And finally John hears "every creature in heaven and on earth and under the earth and in the sea, and all therein" (5:13) adding its voice to the praise of the Father and the Lamb – praise that is concluded with an "Amen" from the four living creatures and homage from the elders.

- What is the central reality of the Universe according to the revelation John was given?
- How should we respond to knowing this?

Summary

John has seen, and given to us, a striking picture of the true nature of God's creation. At the centre is the Father on the throne, accompanied by the Spirit and the Son. Around the throne are the 'throne bearers', the four creatures representing restored creation. Next is the ruling church represented by the twenty-four elders. Beyond this are the millions of angels, and finally every other creature in the whole of creation. Ultimately, creation exists to the praise and glory of God, and in particular his glory in saving mankind from sin (cf Eph 1:6,12,14).

Seals One to Four: The Four Horsemen of the Apocalypse 6:1-8

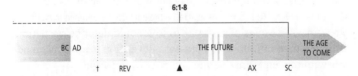

As the Lamb begins to open the seals John sees *the result for the world of God's judgement on human sin.* This judgement is presented from the beginning of Scripture onwards as a *curse* (Gen 3:14, 16-18; Deut 28:15-68, etc.). Coloured horses, and on them terrifying riders, appear in response to a call from each of the four living creatures (6:1,3,5,7). The colours of the horses, and the emblems of the riders, are clearly symbolic and tell us of what each judgement consists:[2]

• The white horse and crown (6:2) symbolize *conquest and victory*, but it is the victory of human kingdoms. (Hendriksen identifies the rider as Christ, but this is unlikely given the obvious link to the other three riders and their collectively destructive nature.) Human history is the history of conquerors and conquests.

• The red horse and sword (6:4) symbolize *strife and warfare*, but it is the wars of nations, not the spiritual warfare of the Christian.

• The black horse and scales (6:5) symbolize *famine and shortages*, but the luxuries (oil and wine) remain plentiful (6:6).

• The pale (literally "greenish-grey") horse, accompanied by Death and Hades (6:8), symbolizes *death and decay* and we are told the many ways in which they come to people.

The key question concerning the riders, however, is whether the disasters which they bring belong *only* to a time immediately before the end of the world. For an answer we should look at passages like Mk 13:5-8 and compare the disasters *there* with the similar disasters in this passage. Jesus said of such disasters that they must happen, "but the end is *not yet*" (Mk 13:7). If we compare these words with the human experience of history we may see that, although things may get worse in the future, the disasters of Rev 6:1-8 are essentially *those which are common to every generation*. The events of seals one to four could describe *any* period from the time of John to the present. Revelation is not concerned *only* with the 'end times' as the Futurists would argue.

However, the power which the riders have is "given" to them (6:2,4,6 & 8) – it is not something they have as of right. Moreover, they come out at the *command* of each of the living creatures around the throne of God. The implication is that the world's disasters are *ultimately under God's control*. Indeed, however

2. See G D Fee & D Stuart *How to Read the Bible for All It's Worth* (London: Scripture Union, 1983) p 214.

puzzling it may seem to us, one of the central messages of Revelation is that *God is ultimately in control of everything*. The *sufferings* of the world are, first and foremost, consequences of Divine *judgement* on the world – but because they are under God's control they will not last forever (cf Rom 8:20)!

- How do you respond to the idea that nothing happens in the world without the permission of God?
- Why does Revelation spend so much time on the problem of suffering?
- Does Revelation provide an answer to the problem of suffering?

The Fifth Seal: The Saints Under the Altar 6:9-11

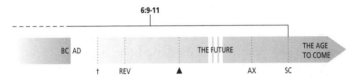

John now mentions for the first time an "altar" (6:9 - 8:3 tells us its position was "before the throne"). Under it (perhaps where the blood of sacrifices was poured out, Lev 4:7) he sees "the souls of those who had been slain for the word of God and for the witness" (Greek, *marturian*, from which we get the word martyr) "they had borne" (6:9, cf 3:8). These souls should perhaps be seen as representing persecuted Christians, epitomized by those who had been killed for their faith. We should bear in mind that Revelation concerns "what must soon take place" (1:1), so that this vision need not necessarily describe *past* martyrs. However, we should probably see it as including *all* God's people slain for their faithfulness (cf Matt 23:34-35). This is not necessarily a vision of the results of some *future* 'great persecution'. The point is rather that there is an element of suffering general to the world (including Christians), described under the opening of the first four seals, and there is another element of suffering, to which more attention will be given as the book develops, which is specific to God's people.

The words of the saints convey a sense of impatient waiting for God to judge "those who dwell upon the earth" and to "avenge" their blood (6:10). This should not be seen as a desire for personal revenge so much as *a desire for the vindication of the gospel for which they had died* (cf Matt 23:29-36). Like the unbeliever, the believer is also driven to ask God why he permits suffering to continue in the world. However, the answer in both cases is the same – he is waiting "until the number of their fellow servants and their brethren should be complete, who were to be killed as they themselves had been" (6:11, cf 2 Pet 3:9). This is a remarkable statement about the sovereignty of God in history. He not only controls the timing of judgement, but does so in order that the full number of saints may be brought into the kingdom! It also tells us, however, that *the experience of the church in a world under judgement will be one of suffering.* Meanwhile, these souls are given white robes as a sign of victory and cleansing from sin (6:11, cf 7:14; Isa 1:18). Thus those who have 'endured to the end' (Matt 10:21-22) are secure (cf 14:13; Phil 1:23), but they have not yet received the *fullness* of the hope which we all have in him. For this they must wait patiently until the resurrection and final judgement.

The Sixth Seal: The End of the World and the "Sealed" of God
6:12-7:17

The phenomena which accompany the opening of the sixth seal in 6:12-17 are associated elsewhere in Scripture with the end of the world (Isa 34:4; Joel 2:30-31; Hag 2:6-7 etc., cf Mk 13:24-27, Matt 24:27-31). It is particularly clear from 6:15-17 that this is the *Day of Judgement* – the great day of the wrath of God and the Lamb. However, John's vision does not simply conclude at this point! Instead, a vital question is posed: "the great day of their wrath has come, and *who can stand before it?*" (6:17).

The vision now proceeds to answer this question. John sees four angels who are told "Do not harm the earth or the sea or the trees, till we have sealed the servants of our God upon their foreheads" (7:3). But we would expect that the events of 6:12-14 would have already done considerable damage to the land, sea and trees! *This is a fundamental indication that events which follow one another in the NARRATIVE of Revelation do not always follow one another in TIME.* In fact, the sealing of the servants of God must have taken place *before* the sequence beginning in 6:1. It is what we would call a "flash-back". The verb for "sealing" is from the same root as the noun for the "seals" in 5:1 etc. The action being referred to is *the setting aside of God's elect to keep them secure in the Day of Judgement.* These people have been sealed in Christ, not merely before the world was destroyed, but before it *began* (cf 17:8; Eph 1:4,13; Matt 24:31 – noting the parallel reference to the "four winds").

The events of 7:1-7 stand before and after time

John *heard* the *number* of those who were sealed: "a hundred and forty-four thousand sealed, out of every tribe of the sons of Israel" (7:4 – see below for an explanation of this number). What he *sees*, however, is "a great multitude which no man could number" (7:9). The number of his people is surely known to God, as indicated by the tribes and round numbers of vv.3-8 (cf Rom 11:25). But to the human observer they are an innumerable host (cf Gen 15:5) "from every nation, from all tribes and peoples and tongues". The answer to the question posed in 6:17 is that *these* can stand "before the throne and before the Lamb" with the white robes and palm branches of victory. And they can do this, not because of their own righteousness, but because *"Salvation* belongs to our God... and to the Lamb" (7:10).

The picture of heaven seen at the end of chapter 5 now takes on a new dimension. The symbolic 'eternal' church of the twenty-four elders is joined by the actual *historical* church of the innumerable multitude whose position "before the throne" (7:9) is within the circle of the elders (cf 4:5 where the seven lamps are similarly "before the throne"). Another outburst of homage is prompted by their cry of praise (7:11). These people are simply the saints of every generation. They have come through the tribu-lation which is the condition of John and his audience (7:14, cf 1:9). They have benefitted from the blood of the Lamb which redeems every believer (cf 5:1b). They are the kingdom of God's priests, which is the present *and* future condition of God's people (cf 1:6; 5:9-10). Now, however, they will not suffer again. Instead, they will be lead into all good things by the Lamb who is their shepherd (7:17). Much of the imagery in 7:15-17 reflects that of 21:3-4, which confirms that we are given here a foretaste of the end. Thus the picture of world history which began at 6:1 ends with the redemption of God's people.

THE 144,000

This number is a source of much confusion, not least to Jehovah's Witnesses who believe it represents a 'special category' of Christians, separate from and more privileged than the 'run of the mill' believer. This suggestion must be rejected, not least because, when we compare 7:4-8 with the other passage where the 144,000 are mentioned (14:1-5), they all appear to be male Jewish virgins! Their meaning is clearly symbolic, and a clue to their real nature lies in the fact that in the list of the twelve tribes given in 7:4-8, one of the tribes of the Patriarchs (Dan) is missing, and Manasseh, the son of Joseph, has taken his place. This reminds us of the fate of Judas who, though he was among the original twelve Apostles, fell away and was replaced by another (cf Acts 1:20). Moreover, in the New Testament the status previously given to Israel is applied to the church (cf Rom 11:25-26a; Jas 1:1; 1 Pet 1:1-2; 2:9-10). Twelve being the number of the tribes and apostles, and 1,000 representing the 'most superlative' number, then 144,000 (12 x 12 x 1,000), symbolizes the vast and complete number of all the people of God under the Old and New Covenants.

The Seventh Seal: Silence in Heaven 8:1

When the seventh seal is opened nothing more is said, but rather there is "silence in heaven for about half an hour". There is a sense in which silence, not praise, is the ultimate response to God (cf Hab 2:20), for his is the 'last word' and he sustains us, rather than the other way round (cf Acts 17:24-25).

Summary

The section from 4:1–8:1 has taken us through the whole sweep of Creation and History. It has shown us the ultimate reality in the heavenly 'Throne Room' and the proper relationships with God which lie at the heart of existence. It has shown us that the central problem of the world is sin, and has shown how this has been resolved by Christ, the Lamb who was slain. It has shown us how, through the everyday world of suffering as a result of judgement on sin, God is working to bring about his purposes of redemption. Finally, it has shown us history being brought to its proper resolution with the judgement of the world of sin, and the glorification of God's people.

■ THE SEVEN TRUMPETS 8:2-11:18

The end of the world and the restoration of all things might seem a good place for the book of Revelation to stop, and the "silence in heaven" certainly provides a pause. However, the vision continues, and we need to ask why. In this next section John seems to be seeing similar things to those described previously, but *from a different perspective*. As 4:1–8:1 has given us the whole summary of human history and the purposes of God, we must assume that the vision resumes *because there are details concerning these matters of which we need to be made more aware*. The following chapters of Revelation are like 'action replays' of a football match, showing the same event but from a different camera angle to bring out new significances.

Preparing to Sound the Trumpets 8:2-6

The next section of the vision opens with more 'sevens' – seven angels and seven trumpets (8:2). Another angel stands before the altar of incense (8:3, cf Ex 40:5). The saints under the altar, seen in 6:9, had been praying for the vindication of the gospel. Now, the angel is assisting their prayers (incense being a symbol of prayer, cf 5:8). The image is similar to that in Rom 8:16-17, where the Holy Spirit is said to help us with our prayers and it is a reminder that our prayers are never *merely* our own. And now the prayers are dramatically answered when the angel casts fire from the altar down on the earth (8:5a, cf Lk 12:49), indicating that God is about to act in judgement. Familiar symbols of God's presence are seen and heard (8:5b, cf 4:5), and the seven angels prepare to sound their trumpets.

Trumpets One to Four: Judgements of Warning on the Earth
8:7-12

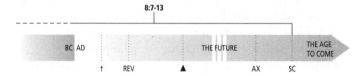

Like the four horsemen of 6:3-8, the first four trumpets are grouped together and bring disasters upon the earth. However, whereas the four horsemen affected the world of mankind, here it is primarily the world of nature which is affected – the earth, sea, fresh waters and even the heavens (cf Gen 1:6-19; Rev 7:2). Man's sin is, nevertheless, the cause of these judgements (cf Gen 3:17b) and his well-being is affected through them (8:9,11). The damage is both devastating and yet partial, "one third" of each area affected being destroyed.

The Purpose of the Judgements 8:13
John then sees and hears an eagle (KJV has "an angel") in the sky. In the Old Testament the eagle was a symbol of power and speed, and was particularly a metaphor for 'swiftly approaching judgement' (e.g. Jer 48:40; Hab 1:8). Certainly the message here is one

---

ECOLOGICAL DISASTERS AND THE END OF THE WORLD

The opening of the first four seals and trumpets brings about a sequence of what we today would describe as 'ecological disasters'. The question therefore arises whether current ecological disasters indicate that the end of the world is imminent. In the past, earthquakes, famines and disease could only be linked indirectly to the fall of man. Today, deforestation, the extinction of animal species, global warming, etc, are much more obviously linked to our impact on the environment. In this sense, these disasters can be seen more clearly than ever before to be a consequence of human sin, and therefore to be warnings of judgement to come (cf Rom 8:19-23). However, there is no way of knowing whether Christ's return is just around the corner or centuries in the future. Ecological disasters tell us we are heading towards the Second Coming, but they do not tell us how far down the road we must yet travel. The thing to remember is that Christians should be encouraged rather than frightened by this knowledge (Lk 21:26-28).

of judgement and we can compare the eagle's words with those of Jesus in Matt 11:20-21. In both cases there is a pronouncement of "woe". In Matthew it is because people have failed to respond to God's blessings, as seen in Jesus' miracles. In Revelation, it is because people fail to respond to God's curses, seen in the world's suffering. Yet such is human nature that neither blessings nor curses readily move us to respond in repentance and faith, even though that is their essential purpose in each case.

The Fifth Trumpet (and First 'Woe'): Demonic Torment 9:1-12

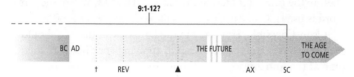

The 'fallen star' John sees next seems to signify Satan (9:1, cf Isa 14:12; Lk 10:18). If this is so, then the one given the keys to the pit is Satan himself, but (as with the four horsemen) his power is limited precisely because it is given to him. According to the book of Revelation, the existence of Satan, sin and suffering do not indicate that the world is out of control. Rather, they are forces God uses to bring about his own purposes (see also 17:17). Thus, although the significance of the "five months" during which Satan acts (9:5) is difficult to determine exactly, its short period surely indicates the divine limitation of Satan even when he apparently has a 'free hand'.

With the key he is given, Satan releases "locusts" from the "bottomless pit" (9:3). Some recent interpreters suggest that John is describing the tanks, planes and helicopters of modern warfare (cf 9:7-10), but although this is an exciting interpretation we have to reject it as fanciful. The "locusts" do not harm the environment but only non-Christians (9:4 cf 7:4), and even then they cannot kill them (9:5). These would be very strange tanks or guns! In any case, their "king" is "Abaddon" or "Apollyon" (9:11) – titles which mean "Destruction" and "Destroyer", and which seem to suggest a demonic head.

The background to this passage is, in fact, the book of Joel, which uses locusts as an image of judgement "before the great and terrible day of the LORD comes" (Joel 2:31 cf 1:4,6; 2:4).

Rather than modern weapons, we should understand the creatures John sees to be those demonic forces which *lie behind* the afflictions of mankind. However, as with the first five seals, there are some forms of suffering which are general to all mankind and others which are specific to certain groups. The fifth seal revealed the souls of the servants of God (6:9). Now the fifth trumpet reveals a worse fate for the enemies of God. As the church suffers the persecution of the world, so the world suffers the torments of Satan (9:5-6, cf 1 Cor 5:5). Yet, interestingly, in the Gospels the demons complain that Christ has come to "torment" them "before the time" (cf Matt 8:29; Mk 5:7; Lk 8:28, where the same word is used). One day the boot will be on the other foot!

It is just possible, especially in the light of v.6, that we should see these verses and the next section applying specifically to the time of the Antichrist (the final outburst of Satanic rebellion against the coming rule of God). In that case the reference to "five months" would correspond to the "one hour" of 17:12, or the "short time" of 20:3. (It has also been suggested that it simply corresponds to the length of the 'locust season'.) What is absolutely clear, however, is that the woes they threaten do not affect Christians. But there is still worse to come!

The Sixth Trumpet (and Second 'Woe'): Demonic Destruction and the Task of the Church 9:13-11:14

The Euphrates runs from Northern Syria down through the territory of *Babylon*, and so symbolizes the boundary between Israel and the ancient enemies of God (cf Gen 11:1-9). Four angels are "bound" there (9:14, i.e. 'restrained from acting', cf 2 Thess 2:7). The sixth trumpet, however, is the signal for their release at the time determined by God (9:15). The very specific nature of this time strongly suggests we are looking at a future event associated with the period of the Antichrist. It is accompanied by further demonic activity, or perhaps even an increase in the powers of the previous forces (9:17-19 cf 9:7-10). The tails of the horses John sees (9:17) are serpents' heads with the power to wound (9:19), which reminds us of an earlier serpent in Eden (Gen 3:15). But for just this reason we may assume that this demonic horde has no power to "wound" God's people (cf Lk 10:19, where this verb is translated "hurt").

However, there is no protection for the rest of mankind. Unlike the former demonic horde which had power only to torment, these have the power to kill by means of their "plagues" (9:18) – although still only a proportion ("a third") of mankind. Yet the effect of this second 'woe' is again that people will not repent. Instead, they go on sinning, against *God* through idolatry (9:20), and against *one another* through murder, fornication and theft (9:21). The lesson of this whole section is of the hardness of the human heart in spite of God's warnings (cf Jer 18:11-12).

- How does the emphasis in the section from 9:1-21 (the sixth trumpet) compare with 6:9-17 (the sixth seal)?
- What is the reason given here for the sufferings of the world?
- How should Christians respond to the sufferings of non-Christians? (Does it just 'serve them right ?)

The Commissioning of the Prophet 10:1-11

The emphasis in this section is on the world which is opposed to God. We therefore need to understand *how the church relates to that world* in the time before the end. Thus John now sees "another mighty angel", distinct from the angels having the trumpets, "coming down from heaven" (10:1). His appearance has some of the characteristics of the earlier vision of Christ and of God (cf 1:15, 4:3). Also his voice reminds us of the voice of God (10:3 cf Amos 1:2). It therefore seems that this angel *speaks on behalf of, and with the authority of, God himself.*

However, John is specifically told *not* to reveal what the seven thunders have said (10:4). In contrast to the rest of the book, this is to be sealed up (cf Dan 12:4,9). However, unlike with Daniel, this is not a sealing up for later revelation. The words are not even to be written down! There are some heavenly things "which man may not utter" (2 Cor 12:4). Our problem is that we are often more interested in *these* things than the message God has given us for the world (cf Rev. 22:10). John hears that there should be "no more delay" (10:6, cf 6:10) because the time is at hand when "the mystery of God, as he announced [the word literally means 'evangelized'] to his servants the prophets, should be fulfilled". This "mystery" is simply *the gospel* (cf Eph 3:4-6, 1 Pet 1:10-12), and it is to be "fulfilled" in that *judgement and redemption are about to come* (cf Acts 10:42-43; 17:30-31). It would be a great help in our generation if we were less curious about the 'heavenly revelations' of modern so-called prophets and more urgently interested in the gospel.

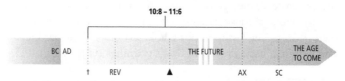

The sixth trumpet has sounded, the end of the world and the judgement are just around the corner, but before then there is a job to do. The giant angel has been carrying a "little scroll" (10:2) – "little" because, as we now see, John is to eat it (10:9). Ezekiel also ate the scroll containing the words of God's judgement and found it sweet in his mouth (Ezek 3:1-3, cf Psa 119:103). John, however, finds the scroll is bitter in his stomach (10:10). The word of God has a bitter quality because it brings *judgement* as well as *salvation* (cf Jer 20:7-9). Once John has eaten, he is ready to prophesy about (i.e. "preach God's word to") the whole world (10:11).

The Two Witnesses 11:1-14
As in the case of the sixth seal, however, the sequence of events is now interrupted to take us back in time (cf 7:1-8) in order to consider the situation of the church. John is given a measuring rod and told to measure the inner sanctuary of the temple (Greek: *naos*), the altar and (literally) those who honour God there, but to exclude everything else – even the outer part of the temple – "for it is given over to the nations". For a similar example of 'measurement', we can compare Ezek 40:3–42:20. There it occurs at the start of a passage which symbolizes *the restoration of God's people after their exile*. Here, it symbolizes *the security of God's people in a world under judgement* (cf Eph 2:19-22; 1 Pet 2:5,9,11-12).

Outside this sanctuary lies everyone who comes under judgement. These are the "nations", (i.e. the Gentiles) whose "times" will last forty-two months (cf Lk 21:24).

On the basis of a stylized 'month' of thirty days, this period of forty-two months equals 1,260 days, which is half of seven years. Hence the times of the Gentiles are deliberately cut short, and day by day during the whole of this period the "two witnesses" will declare God's word to the unbelieving world (11:3). The language of 11:4 is similar to that used of Zerubbabel and Joshua, respectively the anointed King and Priest, in Zech 3-4. The image of Priest and King is appropriate because *the church is made up of God's priests and kings in the world* (cf 5:10). The fact that there are two of them also points to their *missionary activity* (cf Mk 6:7; Lk 10:1) and their *reliability* (cf John 8:17-18). They wear sackcloth because they have responded to, and now preach, the gospel of *repentance* (11:3, cf Matt 11:21). They have power to burn up their enemies, and perhaps in John's vision they literally did. However, a comparison with Jer 5:14 shows us that the destruction they bring is symbolic of *the condemnation God's word brings to a sinful world.* The signs of 11:6 indicate that they preach in the power of Elijah and Moses, the archetypal prophet and lawgiver of the Old Testament. It was also Elijah and Moses who appeared with Jesus on the mount of transfiguration and Lk 24:27 reminds us that *the law and the prophets point to Jesus and the gospel.* Thus the two witnesses John sees may be taken as representing the witness to Jesus born by God's people in the world.

This preaching ministry of the church will continue successfully as long as God permits (11:7). However, in spite of their power, the ultimate fate of the witnesses is to be killed when "the beast that ascends from the bottomless pit" attacks them (11:7). This "beast" is probably to be identified with the "star" in 9:1, and certainly with Satan in 20:7 (cf 17:8), and we are probably, therefore, talking about the time of the Antichrist. It would appear that at this stage in world history the witness of the church will be effectively stifled, though whether by indifference or persecution remains to be seen. The place where the witnesses are killed is in the holy city itself (11:8, cf 11:2) and a comparison with Lk 13:33-35 reminds us that opposition to God is often found where it should be least expected.

The great irony of the gospel is the strenuous efforts to which people of every race and religion go in trying to refute its good news. The response of the nations to the end of the gospel witness is rejoicing (11:10), because the testimony of the witnesses has been a torment to them. Sadly, the gospel is always a torment to an unbelieving world (cf 2 Cor 2:15-16), and the world rejoices whenever the true voice of the church is silenced. However, after "three and a half days" (a short time – half of seven days) the witnesses are resurrected (11:11-12). God will vindicate his people, particularly at Christ's return (cf 1 Pet 4:4-5). Meanwhile, the individual Christian can be killed but never destroyed (cf Matt 10:28). The world, however, is a different matter. The city is judged and "seven thousand" are killed in the subsequent earthquake (11:13). And even at this stage, as we so often find, the death of the witnesses is not wasted and their resurrection produces some response in an unbelieving world.

- What is the task of the church before Christ's return?
- How can we avoid being distracted from this task?
- What distractions are presented to Christians, and how does the book of Revelation show them to be distractions?

The Seventh Trumpet: The Reign of God 11:15-18

At last, the seventh trumpet sounds. Unlike the seventh seal, which was followed by an awesome silence in heaven, however, the seventh trumpet provokes "loud voices" (11:15). Suddenly, the world is put to rights – the old things pass away, and the "kingdom of our Lord and of his Christ" is ushered in. God, who was described in 1:8 as the one "who is and who was and who is to come", is now simply the one "who is and who was" because, at last, *he has come!* Ironically, however, the beginning of God's reign (11:15-17) is in fact the time of the third "woe", as a comparison of 11:18 with Psalm 2 will show. The 'rage' of the nations in rejecting the rule of God and Christ is ultimately in vain. Now the judgement described here brings reward for the saints but punishment for those whose sin had included and exacerbated the destruction of God's world (11:18).

Summary
Once again, we have covered the whole of world history up to Jesus' Second Coming and the establishment of God's Kingdom. However, whereas in the previous section the emphasis was on the saints, and particularly on their security in the middle of a troubled world, in this section the emphasis has been on the world opposed to God, and on the church's relationship with it. The role of the church in the time before the end is to preach the gospel in spite of the fact that it is unwelcome and that to do so will invite persecution and suffering.

■ THE HOLY WAR 11:19-15:4

The Temple Opened – the Saints Secure 11:19
There is a new 'opening' here (cf 4:1; 15:5; 19:11). The connecting "and" (omitted by NIV) in 12:1 suggests that the next section of Revelation begins at 11:19, and it runs right through to 15:4. John sees the interior of the *heavenly* "temple" (cf Heb 8:1-5 – the word refers to the inner 'Holy of Holies'), and in it the ark of the covenant. The earthly ark was lost in the time of the Babylonian Exile (586BC). That the ark is now seen in the heavenly temple, however, indicates that God's covenant with man can *never* be 'lost' (cf Col 3:3). The saints of God 'dwell secure', and this is of crucial importance in this section of Revelation which concentrates on the church's warfare on earth. The vision of the ark is, as so often in Revelation, accompanied by awesome signs of God's presence related to the experience of Israel at Mt Sinai where the covenant was affirmed (Ex 19:16-19).

'Signs' of Conflict: The Woman and the Dragon 12:1-6

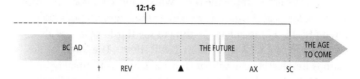

The scene then moves to a 'tableau' in heaven — "a great portent" (literally, a "*sign*") appears (12:1). The character of a sign is that it signifies something, and it is actually fairly obvious what the woman signifies. She is accompanied by the symbols of ancient Israel — the sun, moon and stars stand for Joseph's father, mother and brothers in his dream (Gen 37:9-10) — and she is therefore a sign for God's people. The significance of her *pregnancy* (12:2) goes back to the curse on the serpent after the Fall (Gen 3:15). There, Satan was told that the woman would give birth to one who would "bruise" his head. So the woman is also a sign of the coming deliverer, i.e. the Messiah (cf Lk 10:19). But until the birth of Jesus, the prophets looked in vain for a child who would be born to fulfil this promise (cf Isa 26:17-18).

This also helps us understand the second sign John then sees — "a great red dragon, with seven heads and ten horns, and seven diadems upon his heads" (12:3). The dragon is clearly Satan (cf 12:9). Then, if red symbolizes *strife*, seven indicates *completeness*, and ten *a great number*, whilst heads stand for *authority*, horns for *power* and diadems (or crowns) for *rule*, what we have here is one who causes strife yet with complete authority, great power and complete rule. It is a terrifying picture of the one whom Paul calls "the god of this world" (2 Cor 4:4). And if the fallen star in 9:1 indicates Satan's own fall from heaven, then the mention of "a third of the stars" in 12:4 suggests that he brought many angels down with him.

In John's vision, the dragon is waiting to devour the woman's child. In the light of Gen 3:15 we understand that this pictures Satan hoping to destroy the one who, it has been promised, will otherwise destroy him. However, Satan's plan fails (cf Matt 2:1-18). 12:5 gives us 'a brief history of the Incarnation'. The Messiah is born (cf Psa 2:8-9), and is "caught up" to heaven (for the same verb, cf 2 Cor 12:2,4), where he rules with God.

But whilst their Lord reigns in heaven, what happens to the

people of the Messiah on earth? A constant theme of John's vision is that the security of the church is guaranteed. Thus although the woman is not snatched up with her child, in the period between Christ's ascension and his return (1,260 days, cf 11:2,3), she flees into "the wilderness" (12:6) "where she has a place prepared by God". There is a parallel here with the experience of Elijah, who was nourished by God in the wilderness (1 Ki 17:1-3), and also with that of the Israelites under Moses. In Exodus 3:12 the wilderness was depicted as the place where God's people would serve him after leaving Egypt (cf Rev 11:8, where "Egypt" is the symbol of the sinful world). And the New Testament people of God also live in the 'wilderness' (cf 1 Cor 10:1-13; Heb 3:7-13). All this indicates that, in spite of Satan's raging, the church shares the security of her Lord because she is cared for by God himself and is able to go on serving him in the time before Christ's return.

The War in Heaven – and its Results on Earth 12:7-17

One of the curious features of the Old Testament is that Satan seems to have a place in heaven (cf Job 1:6). In John's vision we again see that this was once the case. But we also see it was not a situation which was allowed to continue indefinitely. Consequent on the Incarnation (12:5), there is a war in heaven: "Michael" (the angelic champion of God's people, cf Dan 10:13,21; 12:1; Jude 9) "and his angels" fight against and expel "the dragon and his angels" (12:7-9). Notice here a reminder that, whilst God alone determines what happens, the instruments of God's will are often his angels (cf Psa 103:20). And here, at last, Gen 3:1 is made clear and the "ancient serpent" is exposed as Satan himself.

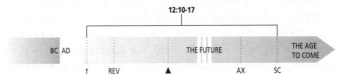

We have linked this 'casting down' of Satan with the Incarnation of Jesus (cf Mk 3:23-27; Lk 10:18-19; Jn 12:31). However, we cannot isolate any one incident in Jesus' life or ministry as bringing about Satan's downfall. Rather, the whole of his Incarnation is the action which brings it about, though perhaps from 12:5 we should see the Ascension of Christ after his victory on the cross as the final 'clinching' action (cf Eph 4:8). But the heavenly victory over Satan is not confined to the Lord of the church nor to his angels. Satan constantly accuses Christians of sin – and does so before God himself (12:10) – but they also share their Lord's victory. Two elements contribute to this (12:11): "the blood of the Lamb" (i.e. Jesus' death on the cross) and "the word of their testimony" (i.e. a life lived in obedience to the gospel, cf Rom 10:9). That they "loved not their lives even unto death" (12:11) is not a third element but is the evidence of this obedience to the gospel (cf Mk 8:34-38, etc.). Notice, victory in 'spiritual warfare' is not achieved by special people or special methods. Satan is overcome by the outworking of the gospel in the life of the ordinary Christian (cf Rom 16:20, Jas 4:7, 1 Pet 5:8-9). No wonder there is rejoicing in the heavens (12:12), when it is seen how the church on earth is doing!

However, there is one aspect of the heavenly victory over Satan which is bad news. Knowing that "his time is short" (12:12), he is determined to take out his fury on the world. His rage is particularly directed against the church, but it will not succeed because God protects her. In John's vision, she is given "the two wings of the great eagle" to fly to the wilderness (12:14). This is another reference to the Exodus (Ex 19:4) and God's saving acts. But the wilderness is a place of both security and testing (Psa 95:8-11, cf 1 Cor 10:1-13; Heb 3:7 – 4:16). The three-and-a-half years ("a time, and times and half a time", 12:14) that the woman is in the desert is the same as the 1,260 days of 12:6, or the 42 months of 11:2. Thus for the whole of the time before Christ's return there will always be a church, and it will always be ultimately secure, but it will also always be a church under testing.

Unable to catch the woman, the dragon tries to drown her with a river of water from his mouth (12:15). The imagery of this section is difficult. Hendriksen and Caird both relate it to the "stream of lies" put out by the Devil, but there may be more to it than this. There is a complex association in the Bible between the ground on the one hand and on the other hand God's curse on human sin (e.g. Gen 3:17; 5:29), blood as a means of cleansing (e.g. Lev 17:11-13) and water as having associations with blood (e.g. Deut 12:16; 2 Sam 23:13-17). In particular, in Gen 4:10-11 Cain is told by God that, "the voice of your brother's blood is crying to me from the ground. And now you are cursed from the ground, which has *opened its mouth* to receive your brother's blood from your hand." Perhaps, therefore, the river of water in Revelation 12 symbolizes the blood of those Satan killed in his attempt to destroy the church. It may also refer to the blood of Jesus, whose death Satan might have thought would put an end to God's plan of salvation (cf 1 Cor 2:7-8).

Whatever the case, Satan does not succeed. Yet the security of the church as a whole is no guarantee of the peaceful existence of any individual member. The dragon, frustrated in his attempt to destroy the woman, goes off "to make war on the rest of her offspring, on those who keep the commandments of God and bear testimony to Jesus" (12:17) – that is, on *ordinary Christians*. John next sees the instruments Satan uses in his warfare against the church. The dragon stands on the seashore, between the sea and the land (cf the angel in 10:2), and out of each arises a fantastic beast.

Satan's Weapons: (1) Political Powers 13:1-10

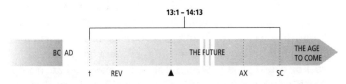

The background to this section is Daniel 7. The Hebrews were not great seafarers, and the sea for them was a theological symbol of both chaos (Gen 1:2) and threat (Jer 5:22). For this reason it also came to symbolize the enemies of God (Isa 27:1; 57:20) and the Gentile "nations" (Isa 17:12-13; cf Rev 17:15). The 'beast from the sea' thus suggests that Satan turns first to the world of unbelief to fashion an instrument with which to express his rage and wage war on Christians.

In some respects the beast from the sea is like the dragon of

12:3 (except that its crowns are on its horns – which indicates that it rules 'by strength' – rather than on its heads, which would symbolize rule 'by authority'). Moreover, its power, rule and authority are given to it by the dragon (13:2). Essentially, therefore, its character is *Satanic*. The "blasphemous name" on each head (13:1) underlines this. However, in appearance it is a *combination* of the beasts Daniel saw in his dream (12:2, cf Dan 7:4-7). Since *those* beasts represented *individual* kingdoms (Dan 7:17), we should understand this beast in Revelation as representing political 'powers' in general.

One of the heads of the beast appears to have been mortally wounded, yet it has recovered, which adds to the fascination the beast has for the whole world (13:3). This is less likely to be a reference to the assassination of some world leader who then 'miraculously' revives, as to the 'head crushing' effects on Satan of Christ's crucifixion (cf Gen 3:15) from which Satan seems to have recovered. The true power of Satan was destroyed by the death of Christ (Heb 2:14), yet the beast lives on! There may also be a reference here to the apparent 'indestructibility' of the world system. The world continues the same as ever (cf 2 Pet 3:3-4) and God is marginalized whilst people 'worship' political power. Yet to take this attitude is really to submit to Satan himself (13:4, cf 1 Cor 10:20-21).

Satan is able to exercise his power within the world of unbelief for the period between Christ's first and second comings (cf 13:5). However, the power of the state is, Biblically speaking, neutral and is, in fact, designed by God for good (Rom 13:1-7). It is only in the hands of Satan that it becomes an instrument for evil. The first beast of Revelation 13 is thus not one particular power or state, but all powers and all states when they are manipulated by Satan and supplant God. At such times, the state speaks against God and his people (13:6, cf Dan 7:8). Worse, it is able to *overcome* the church (13:7, cf Dan 7:20-21)! The 'beast' of satanically manipulated political power is thus able to hold sway over the people of the world, particularly when political power is seen as all-important. And, unwittingly, people honour and serve Satan when they come under this influence because they fail to acknowledge God who made them (cf Rom 1:25).

Christians are protected against this error (cf 13:8), but therefore suffer the consequences. And yet they are not entitled to resist the state with the state's weapons. 13:9 begins with God's call to 'pay attention' – "If any one has an ear, let him hear" (cf the use of this phrase by Jesus). The Greek text of 13:10 is rather confusing to us, but it echoes the words of Jer 43:11 to warn Christians that some of them will be imprisoned or even killed in such periods (13:10). This is inevitable, but Jeremiah's prophecy is (in the best texts of Revelation, cf NIV footnote) adapted to include Jesus' warning *against* using the sword, found in Matt 26:52. Whatever the state does to them for their faith, Christians can only "overcome evil with good" (Rom 12:21).

?

- How does our own political system deal with the things of God?
- Is this an example of what Revelation 13:1-10 is warning us against?
- How should Christians resist the state when it opposes the gospel?

Satan's Weapons: (2) False Ideologies 13:11-18
Then John sees a second "beast", this time arising out of the earth (13:11). The appearance of this beast is *particularly deceptive*. It looks rather like a lamb (cf 5:6), but when it opens its mouth we realize it speaks like a dragon (cf 12:9). It thus has the appearance of Jesus, but the voice of Satan! Small wonder that in 16:13 and 19:20 it is described as "the false prophet". This second beast represents false ideology in general and false religion in particular. Its authority (13:12), however, is derived from the first beast of political power, which in turn got its power from Satan (13:1). The reason for this dependency is simply that false ideology in *itself* harms only those who believe it. It needs to be harnessed to the power of the state to do any real damage to the church. We need think only of Hitler's Germany, Mao's China or Khomeini's Iran. As ideologues, Hitler, Mao and Khomeini were merely embittered fanatics. As political rulers, however, they led multitudes to destruction and made life misery for true believers.

The second beast has amazing power which *seems* like the power of God. Indeed, its "horns like a lamb" (13:11) suggest a power like that of Jesus himself (horns being a symbol of power). In particular, it can perform miracles which were the prerogative of God in the Old Testament, such as causing fire to come down from heaven (cf 1 Ki 18:24; 2 Ki 1:10), and making an idol speak (cf Psa 115:5; Jer 10:5). The lesson here is that *spiritual power* is no guarantee of *spiritual truth* (cf Matt 24:24, etc.). Yet Christians need not be unduly alarmed. Our safeguard is the *message*, not the messengers, so that the second beast is betrayed by its *voice* (13:11). If the message is not the gospel of Jesus, the Christian may be sure that the rest is irrelevant (cf Gal 1:8), however impressive it may look.

When false ideology is supported by corrupted state power, however, Christians will always suffer. Sometimes there will be violent persecution (13:15). Quite often, however, it is simply the loss of economic and social privileges, so that in John's vision those who were not slain and yet who did not receive the mark of the beast were unable to engage in normal commerce (13:17). The Christian who cannot get a job, or who misses promotion, as a result of sticking to principles knows what this is about.

The Triumphant Church 14:1-5
John has seen the instruments of Satan's warfare on the church, and the effects they have. He now sees what has happened to the church as a result. The 144,000, first seen in 7:4 and representing the total number of God's people, are still here in 14:1, exactly the same in number in spite of all that Satan has done! Notice they bear the 'mark of the Lamb' – "his Father's name" (14:1) - written on their foreheads (cf 7:3). The origins of this 'mark' are in Ezekiel, where God tells an angelic scribe to "put a mark upon the foreheads of the men who sigh and groan over all the abominations" committed in Jerusalem (Ezek 9:4). People who speculate about the 'mark of the beast' being a physical mark such as a barcode usually ignore this background.[3]

The 'mark of the Lamb' comes first in the Bible and refers to those who belong to God (cf Matt 6:4,6). These are kept safe for eternity (Jn 10:27-30) but you will not be able to detect them in

3. A helpful article by Ivan Sneddon, 'Barcodes, 666 and the mark of the beast' in *Southern Cross* (the newspaper of the Anglican Diocese of Sydney, June 1996, p 13) points out that the number six in a barcode is represented on the left of the code by one space, one bar, one space and four bars, or on the right by one bar, one space, one bar and four spaces. The three 'guard bars', alleged by some to form the number 666, each consist simply of one bar, one space and one bar, whether they appear on the left, right or centre. Their resemblance to sixes is thus entirely superficial.

THE NUMBER OF THE BEAST

Probably more nonsense has been preached and written on the number of the beast than any other passage in Scripture. There have been well over 100 different interpretations of the number 666 (literally "six hundred and sixty and six"), usually on the assumption that the number requires us to *calculate a name*. Such a variety of suggestions, some of which (e.g. 'Oliver Cromwell') were clearly wrong, suggests (a) we don't know what it means, and (b) perhaps we are asking the wrong questions. The *right* answer probably lies in recog-nizing that John tells his audi-ence to "reckon" (cf Lk 14:28) the *number* not the name (13:18). He then seems to give a clue, "it is a human number", and then the answer: "its number is six hundred and sixty-six". The number six is sometimes seen as particularly signifying 'man' because man was created on the sixth day and six days were allocated for his labour. If seven is the perfect number, and three the superlative (cf 4:8) or Divine (Father, Son and Holy Spirit) number, then 777 would be a good number to represent God. 666 is then the number of man pretending to be God (cf Mk 13:14, 2 Thess 2:4) or falling short of God. It is a notable feature of the state-ideology combination that a man emerges whose personality and word dominates the new society in a 'godlike' way. Hitler, Mao and Khomeini have been mentioned, but we could add Stalin, Amin, Ghadaffi, Hussein and many others from the 20th century alone. No doubt the final Antichrist will have the same characteristic and '666' will describe him perfectly.

this life by looking at their heads! Unfortunately, the obsessive attention Christian literature pays to the 'mark of the beast', and the relative ignoring of the 'mark of the Lamb', is an ironic reminder of our fallen nature. Even after conversion, we still find sin more interesting than goodness.

There are also parallels in this passage with Heb 12:22-24 which contrasts the meeting of the church at the spiritual Mt Zion with the meeting of Israel at the physical Mt Sinai. This is particu-larly brought out by the reference to "virgins" in 14:4 (RSV footnote – NIV has, less helpfully, "they kept themselves pure"). Part of the Israelites' preparation for their encounter with God at Sinai was abstention from sexual relations (Ex 19:15). But the 'virginity' of the Lamb's followers in Revelation is not literal, any more than is their Jewishness (cf 7:4-8). Rather, it is representa-tive of their consecration (cf also 2 Cor 11:2). Not even Jehovah's witnesses believe that the 144,000 are literally male Jewish virgins!

14:2-3 also indicates we are back in the heavenly Throne Room of chapters 4 and 5. It is rare, but not unknown, for the church itself (rather than Jesus) to be described as the "first fruits" (14:4b, cf Jas 1:18) However, John is describing in this section not the *qualifications* for redemption (virginity, absolute honesty, sinlessness, etc.) but its *results* (cf Eph 5:25-27 where Christ prepares the bride for himself). In his vision, John is once again seeing the victorious church. It is important, however, that we realize that the 144,000 are just the church of 7:9-10 seen from God's viewpoint (cf 7:4-8). Notice, therefore, that the Lamb whom they follow "wherever he goes" (14:4) is also the "shepherd" of the "great multitude" (7:17).

The Militant Church 14:6-13

However, before the victory is complete, the church has the task of spreading the gospel (cf 11:3-6), which is expressed in three ways by the angels John now sees. The first proclaims the "eternal gospel" (14:6). It is not the gospel of Jesus' death and resurrection as we might recognize it, but it is the *basic* gospel of obedience to the God who is the righteous Judge, which has held true since the time of Adam (14:7, cf Rom 1:20). The second angel brings the declaration of the *effects* of that judgement (14:8). "Babylon" is here introduced without explanation, but we will see more of her shortly. The point made is that, in contrast with the 'virginity' of the saints, the nations have been *seduced* by Babylon's "impure passion". The third angel brings another call for endurance by the saints (14:9-12, cf 1:9, etc.).

There is a particular warning here not to be deluded into following the beast, even when it seems desirable. The price of temporary ease now (14:9, cf 13:17) will be the failure to enter God's rest later (14:11, cf Gen 2:3; Psa 95:11). This message is for the church at *every* point in her history – from "henceforth" (14:13) in the words of the heavenly voice. When tempted to give up on good works because of the hopeless situation around them, Christians should remember the words of the Spirit in 14:13 (cf 1 Cor 15:58).

The Harvest of Life and The Harvest of Judgement 14:14-20

For the background to this part of John's vision, we need to look at Matt 13:24-30 and Jn 4:35-36. The one "seated on the cloud" is (almost certainly) Jesus, both because of his description (14:14) and his distinction from the angels, even though the command for the final in-gathering (14:15) comes to him (via an angel) from the Temple of God. Perhaps this is a graphic

reminder that the knowledge of the final "hour" belongs to the
Father alone (cf Matt 24:36). A comparison with John 4:35,
however, suggests that this harvest includes the fruits of evange-
lism through the whole of history, not just at the Second Coming.
"Another angel" coming from the Temple (14:17, cf 14:15)
harvests the grapes of God's wrath (cf 14:10; Jer 25:15). These
are those who ignore God's warnings given in 14:6-11. The
winepress is outside the holy city (14:20, cf 14:1), showing that
these people have no share in God's inheritance. The distance
given in 14:30 may represent the length of the land "from Dan to
Beersheba", or, as we would say, "from John O'Groat's to Land's
End". The imagery of the winepress, however, is drawn from Isa
63:1-6 and, whilst shocking, is set there in the wider context of
redemption. The negative judgement of God is never an end in
itself, but is part of the process of salvation.

The Saints in Triumph 15:1-4

Though we are nearing the end of this part of the vision, we are
some way from the end of Revelation. John is provided, therefore, with a sign of the 'literary' end by briefly seeing the "seven
angels, with seven plagues, which are the last" (15:1, cf 15:5 –
16:21). They are "another portent" (or "sign", cf 12:1,3) and
shortly we will see what they signify. However, the 'church mili-
tant' of 14:6-13 is now seen as the 'church triumphant' in 15:2.
The saints – "those who had conquered the beast" (15:2, cf
12:11; 13:16-17) – stand by a sea of glass, taking us back yet
again to the heavenly Throne Room of chapters 4 and 5 (cf 4:6).
This sea of glass is perhaps also symbolic of their triumph over the
chaotic sea of 13:1. With their God-given musical instruments

they sing "the song of Moses, the servant of God" (15:3, cf 14:3). The first 'Song of Moses' celebrated God's deliverance of his people from the Egyptians (Ex 15:1-18), so this song also celebrates his deliverance of his people. However, it is also "the song of the Lamb" (15:3) meaning not one sung by him but to him (cf 5:8-10). The song of Rev 15:3-4 celebrates deliverance by the 'servant-king' (cf Isa 42:1, etc.) from the "Egypt" of a world opposed to God (cf 11:8) and expresses the fact that it is God who triumphs, although it is only at the last that his "judgements" are "revealed" (15:4)

Summary
This section showed the heavenly warfare and its earthly counterparts. Satan opposes the church using the instruments of political power and false ideology. At the human level these prevail in their day, but the 'church triumphant' is revealed to John in all its security with its Lord. The task of that church, even in a hostile world, remains to proclaim the gospel and to do good works. At the harvest at the end of the age the final division will take place, and God's wrath will be poured out on those who have opposed him. In eternity the saints will rejoice in their victory over Satan.

◼ THE SEVEN PLAGUES 15:5-16:21

The Sanctuary of the Tent of Witness Opened 15:5-8
John now sees a third "opening" in heaven (15:5, cf 4:1; 11:19), literally an opening of "the sanctuary" (RSV, "temple") "of the tent of witness". The tent Moses built in the wilderness was also called the tabernacle of the testimony, or witness (Ex 38:21). The underlying assumption in Revelation, as we also see in Hebrews, is that the earthly 'shadows' have a heavenly counterpart (Heb 8:5, cf Rev 11:19). However, from the heavenly tabernacle of God there now comes a terrible judgement. In Exodus 40:35 we read that, when the earthly tabernacle was completed, "Moses was not able to enter the tent of meeting, because the cloud abode upon it, and the glory of the LORD filled the tabernacle". Now in Rev 15:8 we see that no one is able to enter the *heavenly* tabernacle until God's judgement is completed. The book of Exodus, with its instructions for building the Tabernacle, is followed by

THE SUB-STRUCTURE OF 15:5-22:21

Chapters 15-22 contain several distinct scenes with an underlying unity. Twice an angel invites John with the words "Come, I will show", the first time introducing Babylon (17:1), the second the New Jerusalem (21:9) and twice more the Sanctuary (15:5 – RSV, "temple") and Heaven (19:11) are "opened". Moreover, the section itself seems to divide into seven (plus an epilogue). The suggested sub-divisions are as follows:

15:5-8	The Sanctuary of the Tent of Witness Opened – the Seven Angels
16:1-21	The Seven Plagues
17:1-19:10	"Come, I will show you" – Babylon
19:11-20:15	Heaven Opened – The Conquering King
20:1-15	The Reigning Saints
21:1-8	The Kingdom of God
21:9-22:17	"Come, I will show you" – Jerusalem
22:18-21	Epilogue

Leviticus, with its instructions for sacrifice and atonement. Throughout the book of Leviticus, the emphasis is on the threat to the Israelites posed by God's holiness: "And if in spite of this you will not hearken to me, but walk contrary to me, then I will walk contrary to you in fury, and chastise you myself sevenfold for your sins" (Lev 26:27-28, cf 10:1-3). And now this terrible warning is fulfilled, not just for unbelieving Israel but for the whole of mankind. We are reminded once again that, though God is a great Saviour, he saves from his own wrathful judgement against sin.

In the plagues which follow (16:1-21) there are parallels with the plagues on Egypt (cf Ex 7:14-10:29). In their context those plagues preceded God's act of deliverance for his people, and so the plagues here in Revelation have been referred to as "the last" (15:1) since what follows will be the final deliverance of the saints. There is also a sense of creation being 'undone'. These plagues are no longer warnings (cf the Seals and the Trumpets) but signs of final judgement. Insofar as these are the last plagues, we should probably think of them as relating mainly to the period of the Antichrist. However, we should not take a 'woodenly literalist' view of their fulfilment. We are still in the realm of John's vision, not modern photo-journalism.

Bowl 1: Unbelievers Judged 16:1-2

The primary targets of God's wrath in this whole section are the unbelievers. Those who do not have the mark of the Lamb (16:2, cf 14:1) have, by definition, the mark of the beast and are servants of him, and, through him, of Satan. These are those people who have either ignored God or who have followed false ideologies. It is appropriate that they are judged in the body, since this is the realm in which they have served evil (cf Rom 1:27).

Bowls 2 and 3: The Sea and the Waters Judged 16:3-7

Previously (8:8-11), only "a third" of the sea and the waters had been affected by judgement. Now the judgement is total. Previously, we saw God's judgements as warnings, now we see them as the final verdict. If the judgements seem harsh to us, the voice of "the angel of waters" (16:5 – RSV, "water") – whose sphere is the very subject of judgement – reminds us that they are entirely deserved and appropriate: "Just art thou in these thy judgments, thou who art and wast, O Holy One. For men have shed the blood of saints and prophets, and thou hast given them blood to drink. It is their due!" (16:5-6). If we remember that drinking blood was absolutely forbidden to God's people in the Old Testament (Gen 9:4, etc.) we will realize that those who (in John's vision) are forced to drink blood are calling down judgement on themselves.

Bowl 4: The Sun Judged and Judging 16:8-9

By contrast with the previous judgement on the sun (8:12), the result of this judgement is not darkness but *scorching heat*. Thus the judged sun itself becomes an instrument of judgement. Even so, since the time for warning is past, the effect of this judgement is not to produce repentance but *to confirm the sinful nature of those judged*. As we see so often in practice, the same suffering which draws some people to God drives others to curse him (16:9), thus revealing much about their relationship with him.

Bowl 5: The Kingdom of the Beast Judged 16:10-11

This effect of this plague with regard to mankind is similar to the last in that *men still do not repent* (16:11). However, we see here that the attacks of God are coming closer to the kingdom of Satan himself.

Bowl 6: The Last Battle 16:12-16

The Euphrates has been mentioned earlier (9:14) as the boundary between God's people and the powers which threaten them. And here, as before, the "kings from the east" (16:12) are more likely to be symbolic than literal. Alex Motyer comments on a similar prophecy in Isaiah 41:2 that, "The situation is unmistakably Palestinian, where every serious turmoil had its origin in the *east* ... in Mesopotamia, and every assailant invaded from the north, along the line of the fertile crescent."[4] As the end nears, so the enemies of God become more frantic in their opposition to him. In the final phase of demonic deception the human kingdoms (16:14) gather – or rather are gathered – against God by repulsive spirits which go out from the *mouths* of the unholy trinity of Satan, the beast and the false prophet (16:13). The close association of word and Spirit in the Bible and the origin of these deceiving spirits suggests that a deceptive message is involved, hence the abiding relevance of 1 Timothy 4:1-2.

Paradoxically, the action of God in removing the barrier to invasion (16:12) *appears* to make the task of his enemies easier, just as it often appears that the world is not under God's control. But it is all by God's will, for the battle to follow is described as being "on the great day of God the Almighty" (16:14) and the words of encouragement in the hour of darkness (16:15) are clearly those of Jesus himself (cf Matt 24:43-44). The response of Christians to all these events must be to stay awake and alert, neither giving up nor becoming complacent in the face of what is happening in the world.

4. J A Motyer *The Prophecy of Isaiah* (Leicester: IVP, 1993) p 309, emphasis in the original.

Satan assembles the armies he gathers at "Armageddon" – a place that has often been identified with the Plain of Megiddo, though there is no *direct* evidence for this (the meaning of the name in Hebrew is simply not clear). But at this stage *the battle is not recorded!* Instead, the vision moves straight to the final judgement.

THE BATTLE OF ARMAGEDDON

Like the number 666, the battle of Armageddon has become a subject of popular curiosity and speculation. However, we must never forget that John is writing of a *vision*. We need not imagine that, at some stage in the future, all the armies of the world will set out with guns, tanks and rockets either to attack Heaven or Jerusalem (cf 20:9). The notion that these armies will one day gather in Israel has led to many fanciful speculations in the past – some of which were clearly wrong because they didn't happen. Armageddon is much more to do with *spiritual*, rather than military, rebellion against God.

Its roots are in passages like Psalm 2:2, "The kings of the earth set themselves, and the rulers take counsel together, against the LORD and his anointed" which are used in the New Testament to talk about resistance to the gospel of Christ (cf Acts 4:23-31).

Bowl 7: The Final Judgement 16:17-21

Instead of describing the final battle, the scene moves abruptly to the final judgement. The lightnings, voices, peals of thunder and earthquake that were seen in the heavenly Temple at the start of the last section (11:19) are now released on the earth. The earthquake signifies here the final 'shaking' of the world (cf Hag 2:6-7; Heb 12:26-27; Rev 11:13). The final act of judgement, however, is a hailstorm worse even than that which afflicted the Egyptians (cf Ex 9:13-35) which again brings out the sinfulness of mankind (16:21).

We might have supposed, particularly from what the voice says in 16:17, that the account of judgement would end here. However, three things prepare us for more to follow. One is that people are described as still unrepentant and cursing God (16:21). We must ask *what finally happens to the impenitent.* The second is another mention of "Babylon" (16:19, cf 14:8). *We need to know more about this city.* Third, we have not yet seen the outcome of the great battle at Armageddon. Although the seven "last" plagues have finished, *we still have some significant 'loose ends' to tie up.*

Summary

The previous judgements on the earth and on mankind were partial, and left room for repentance. God's *last* judgements, however, are total and irrevocable. Eventually the world itself is used as a weapon against the sinner. Yet there comes a point beyond which people will curse God rather than turn to him. We will see that the final condition of the impenitent is simply *impenitence* as they go down fighting the One who created them. The message of this section is that, far from the world being put to rights because people respond to the warnings of God and the preaching of the gospel, it must be brought to destruction because they are impenitent and deserving of judgement.

- Is concern about the environment unnecessary because God will one day destroy the world?
- What is wrong with non-Christian 'Green' attitudes towards environmental problems?

■ THE FALL OF BABYLON 17:1-19:10

We have seen that two of the instruments Satan uses in his warfare against the church are *oppressive politics* (the beast from the sea) and *false ideology* (the beast from the earth). When these combine, the results for the church are dramatic. However, they do not always combine — and meanwhile there is a third instrument which is less dramatic and yet in its way is far more powerful. John's vision now turns to the subject of "Babylon".

Babylon Seen 17:1-6a

John receives an invitation from one of the seven angels from the previous section to come and see "the judgment of the great harlot who is seated upon many waters" (17:1). This, we are told later, is "the great city which has dominion over the kings of the earth" (17:18). The "many waters" on which she is seated indicate the extent of her influence over unbelieving mankind (cf 17:15), but they may also reflect her sense of security (cf Nah 3:8). Her essential character is one of *seduction* and *attraction* which appeals to *all people* (17:2).

Significantly, John is then carried away "in the Spirit" (17:3, cf 1:10) – a reminder that we are in the realm of *visionary*, not *physical*, experience. This journey takes him into "a wilderness" where he sees "a woman" (17:3). Earlier, he had seen another woman (the church – 12:1), in another wilderness (the place of God's security – 12:6). "Babylon" thus has the character of an 'anti-church'. She is *the sum of those who are not God's people*. Since they are not his people, they do not enjoy his security but, as we will see, they trust in a security of their own.

The woman is sitting on a beast which is like the dragon and the beast out of the sea (cf 12:3; 13:1 – see above for the symbolism of the appearance of the beast). From this description we understand that the *ultimate source* of her influence is Satanic. Even so, her own appearance is immensely attractive (17:4a). She is dressed in purple, the colour of civic authority in the Roman empire, and wears fine jewellery. It is only when John sees *inside* the golden cup she is holding that her moral and spiritual character is revealed as one of abominations and sexual impurities (17:4b – we must remember that in the Old Testament, sexual sin was a symbol of *spiritual unfaithfulness*, cf Ezek 16:15-63).

The name written on her forehead (17:5, cf 13:16, 14:1) is literally "Mystery" (RSV, "a name of mystery"), indicating she cannot be understood without divine revelation (cf 1 Cor 15:51, etc.). But the nature of the mystery is then revealed by the rest of her title. The name "Babylon the great" identifies her with mankind's great rebellion against God after the flood (Gen 11:1-9) and the archetypal enemy of God's people in the rest of Scripture. Also she is "mother of harlots and of earth's abominations". This may indicate she is the *origin* of these things. Perhaps more likely, as in Saddam Hussein's famous promise of "the mother of battles", it means she is the *archetype* of them. The Greek word for "harlot", *pornē*, is the root of our own word "pornography" and indicates sexual uncleanness in general as well as the profession of prostitution in particular, but there is undoubtedly a *spiritual* sense to the word here.

Most terrifyingly, however, the woman is "drunk with the blood of the saints and the blood of the martyrs of Jesus" (17:6). (We should remember that "martyrs" here originally simply meant "witnesses".) Being "drunk with blood" indicates she is 'carried away' (cf Deut 32:42) with the persecution of God's people.

The Beast Explained 17:6b-14

John tells us he "marvelled greatly" at his vision (17:6b), probably because of the magnitude of evil the woman represents and her apparent victory over good (cf Dan 7:15). Why does God allow his people to be overcome by the forces opposed to them? As in Daniel, the angel proceeds to explain "the mystery" (17:7), beginning with the beast ridden by the woman (17:8). *The history of the beast is highly significant.* He "was, *and is not,* and is to ascend from the bottomless pit and go to perdition" (17:8). And again John is told, "it was *and is not* and is to come" (17:8). The language indicates a comparison and contrast with God himself "who is and who was and who is to come" (1:4, 8). We already know that the beast is Satanic from its earlier description (17:3, cf 12:3; 13:1). As the woman is the 'Anti-Church', so the beast is the 'Anti-God' and his representative will be the 'Anti-Christ'. But at the time John receives his vision things are neither as bad as they have been nor as bad as they will become, since the beast now "*is not*".

The non-Christian world, that is those "whose names have not been written in the book of life from the foundation of the world" (17:8b), is as impressed by the power of this beast to arise as they were astonished by the revival of the second beast in 13:3-5. Yet they see only that "it was and is not *and is to come*" (17:18c) and appear unaware of the angel's further prediction that the beast will "go to perdition" (i.e. "destruction", 17:8a). There is a play on words here. In 9:11 we were told that the Greek name of the angelic "king" of the bottomless pit was *Apollyon*, which means "Destroyer". But in 17:8 *Apollyon*

(Destroyer) goes to *apōlleian* (destruction). Thus Satan is revealed as ultimately powerless, but in the same verse we are shown how the world displays its ignorance of God's coming judgement. Instead, people continue to be dazzled by Satan's displays of power.

The angel goes on to reveal more things for "a mind with wisdom" (17:9a). Perhaps not surprisingly, therefore, what follows is difficult to interpret! We already know from the earlier visions that the scarlet beast the woman sits on is an image of Satanic authority and power (17:3, cf 12:3). But the angel now talks about the woman being seated on "seven hills" (17:9). It has often been assumed that they correspond to the hills on which the city of Rome was built, and that therefore "Babylon" is a synonym for Rome (or even the Roman Catholic church). However, the Bible generally conceives of hills or mountains (the two are not that distinct) as another symbol of strength or power to rule, particularly in competition with God and his mountain (e.g. Psa 68:15-16, cf Rev 14:1). The seven hills here would then further symbolize the principle of absolute power and rule exalted against God. (Of course, there will be particular examples of this in history, such as the Roman Empire itself at certain stages in its history.) We also need to note that John says literally, "The seven heads are seven hills, where the woman sits on them, and *they* are seven kings". The heads, hills and kings *all* refer to the same concept: *the woman's influence rests on a demonically inspired system of complete authority, power and rule.*

However, there is clearly a future reference here as well. The angel tells John that five of the seven kings have fallen, "one is, the other has not yet come" (17:10). Some interpreters have tried to identify these "kings" with particular emperors or empires. (For example, if we add to the four beasts of Dan 7 – which represent the Babylonian, Medo-Persian, Greek and Roman empires – the Egyptian and Assyrian empires which preceded them, then we need only look for one more 'empire' before the end of the world.) The difficulty with such interpretations, however, is knowing who or what to leave out. There have certainly been *many* empires since the collapse of Rome! We are probably better off understanding the vision to indicate that whilst many powers have fallen, and we live under a 'power' now, there will be one more to come for "only a little while" (17:10). This is again probably a reference to the period of the Antichrist.

In addition to these, the beast itself is described as "an eighth" king who "belongs to the seven" (17:11). He is thus identified with the corrupt rulers of this world who are, in a sense, an extension of the beast. But though he is himself a ruler, he is not present in the world as a king (cf John 12:31).

There are also, however, the "ten horns" which are a further "ten kings" (17:12). This is undoubtedly a reference to the future since they "have not yet received royal power". We have taken "ten" to be a symbol of magnitude and "horns" as a symbol of power (12:3, 13:1). Thus if "kings" symbolize rule, then we have here a situation of *great human power and rule* coexisting "together with the beast" at some time in the future (17:12). Fortunately, this situation will only last "one hour" (cf the "little while" of 17:10, possibly indicating we should identify the rule of the *ten* kings with the rule of the *seventh* king). Again, this seems to refer to the period of the Antichrist, and this interpretation is reinforced by the reference to their "war on the Lamb" (17:14, clearly looking back to 16:12-16). However, in a foretaste of 19:11-21 we are told that this warfare is doomed to failure, for the Lamb is "Lord of lords and King of kings" (17:14) and will therefore conquer his enemies.

The Prostitute Destroyed 17:15-18

Meanwhile, after a glimpse of the future, we return to the prostitute who is *the present manifestation of Satan's influence in the world.* Through her, his influence is global, extending over "peoples and multitudes and nations and tongues" (17:15, cf the redeemed in 7:9). Yet the final instruments of her downfall will be *the agents of Satan himself:* "And the ten horns that you saw, *they and the beast* will hate the harlot; *they* will make her desolate and naked, and devour her flesh and burn her up with fire" (17:16). Why is this so? It seems there are two reasons. One is that though the *instruments* of her destruction are the agents of Satan, the *author* of her destruction is God who has, "put it into their hearts to carry out his purpose" (17:17, note the implied sovereignty of God *even over the wills of his enemies*). But the second reason is surely that, whatever her short term nature (which we will see more clearly in a moment) the fact that "Babylon" is founded on the wickedness of Satan and his followers means that she has built into her the seeds of her own destruction. No social system which is undermined by sinfulness can ever be stable but will always 'self-destruct' (cf Rom 1:28-31).

Judgement Announced 18:1-3

The judgement of "Babylon" is announced by an angel having "great authority" (18:1) – necessary, presumably, for the task in hand. We should note that the words in 18:2 refer not to the *reasons* for "Babylon's" destruction (i.e. *because* she is full of demons, etc.) but to its *results* (cf Isa 13:19-22). The *reasons* for her judgement are given in 18:3 (cf 17:2). Here we begin to see that her attitude to wealth is a crucial part of the character of "Babylon" for which she is condemned.

"And I heard" the judgement of "Babylon" 18:4-24

John then hears a heavenly voice calling God's people to "come out" and have nothing to do with the sins of "Babylon" in order that they may avoid her judgement (18:4). This does not mean Christians should leave the physical world or any particular part of it (cf John 17:15; 1 Cor 5:9-10). Rather, it means living holy lives here and now (cf 1 Cor 5:9-12; 2 Cor 6:14-18). Nor is there a danger, despite the reality of the warning to them, that Christians will come under God's judgement. It is precisely *because* they are his people that they will heed this warning and thus avoid sharing "Babylon's" fate.

The punishment on "Babylon" is described as "double for her deeds" (18:6). Hughes suggests that "the term 'double' here does not mean a twofold amount ... but an exact equivalent, in the same way as a person who looks exactly like someone else is called his double" (p 191). Looked at another way, we might say that the 'sin' plus the 'punishment' equals "double". Hence the voice also says, "As she glorified herself and played the wanton, so give her *a like measure* of torment and mourning" (18:7a).

The essential sin of "Babylon" is finally revealed, however, as *hubris* – an 'overweening pride' – and in particular *the assumption that she will never be judged*. In her heart she boasts "A queen I sit, I am no widow, mourning I shall never see" (18:7b). The passage in Isaiah from which this is a quote reveals Babylon as a "lover of pleasures, who sit securely" (Isa 47:8). But the voice of the angel declares, "mighty is the Lord God who *judges* her" (Rev 18:8).

The Three 'Woes': "Babylon" Revealed 18:9-19

For those who have enjoyed the life of "Babylon", her downfall is a cause for agonized mourning. Three 'woes' are declared over her (cf 8:13). First, "the kings of the earth" mourn the passing of her greatness and power (18:9-10) – and their chance to live in luxury as a result (the word translated "wanton" by the RSV carries the sense of 'luxurious living', cf NEB). Second, "the merchants of the earth" mourn the passing of her "great wealth" (18:11-17a) – and with it their own. Finally, "all shipmasters and seafaring men, sailors and all whose trade is on the sea" – the entrepreneurs in the 'high risk, high return' business of their day – mourn the loss of their opportunities to grow rich (18:17b-19).

Thus *by these three pronouncements, "Babylon" is unmasked*. The first Babylon ("Babel", Gen 11:1-9) was the result of a mighty spiritual rebellion against the God of heaven. The second Babylon was a great empire and the historical enemy of Israel. The last "Babylon", however, is far more mundane. Neither spiritual nor global aggrandizement are her main concern, but political power, luxury and making a 'fast buck' (regardless of the cost in human misery – note the reference to the slave trade in 18:13b). Where the first Babylon shook a fist at God, and the second shook a fist at the world, the third is simply turned in on itself in its desire for more of everything to do with influence and materialism. The success of the final "Babylon", as far as Satan is concerned, is that she seduces people away from an interest in God and blunts their concern about the consequences of their actions by overwhelming them with immediate opportunities for 'the good life'. (This point, incidentally, seems well understood by Muslims in their suspicion of 'the West', but is frequently lost on Christians in spite of the warnings in Mk 4:18-19 etc.).

A Foretaste of Rejoicing 18:20

The punctuation of the RSV is unhelpful at this point. The words of the sailors finish at the end of 18:19. Now a *different* voice – probably that of 18:4 – sounds the first note of joy over "Babylon's" fall. By contrast with the kings, merchants and sailors, the "saints and apostles and prophets" rejoice at the downfall of the institution which treated them so badly (cf 17:6). The phrase used is literally "God has judged your judgement from her" and it carries the sense of God reversing the judgement of "Babylon" on those she condemned.

"Babylon" Remembered 18:20-24

Much of the imagery and language in this section is drawn from Jeremiah's prophecy against Babylon in his own day (Jer 50-51, e.g. 51:45, cf Rev 18:4). As Jeremiah's messenger threw his scroll, tied to a stone, into the Euphrates to symbolize the fall of historical Babylon (Jer 51:63-64), so in John's vision "a mighty angel" throws "a stone like a great millstone" into the sea to declare the fall of this spiritual "Babylon" (18:21). And yet, when we read the section describing "Babylon's" final fate (18:22-24), the picture which emerges is of a society much like our own. This "Babylon" was not a place of Satanic excess but of culture, craft, domestic work, home comforts and normal daily pleasures (18:22-23a). But at the same time, she was inherently corrupt. Her "great men" were not philosophers or spiritual leaders but the money-makers (18:23b), and though her fault was not to destroy the nations in wars, it was, nevertheless, to deceive them (18:23c). She was indeed violent (18:24), but it was violence against those who stood in the way of her pursuit of luxury and the 'good life'. In fact, this "Babylon" (unlike the world of the beast and the false prophet) is characteristic of the Western world today and of every Godless society throughout history.

"Babylon" is thus nothing more, but also nothing less, than the *Godless world order*. We see her clearly today in the prosperous West, but she has cast her spell over all the nations (18:23b). Wherever people are more concerned about power and wealth than about God, or where they see religion as the *means* to power and wealth (cf 1 Tim 6:5), there "Babylon" holds sway. However, because she is Godless she is unable to contain the sinfulness of her own citizens. As every news bulletin shows, the threat to "Babylon" is the violence and lawlessness of the children she creates. Thus it is these who will eventually be the instrument of her downfall (cf 17:16).

- How do you respond to the suggestion that "Babylon" is seen in contemporary society?
- How, as Christians, should we respond to our society's emphasis on material possessions and progress?

Rejoicing in heaven 19:1-5

The fall of Babylon, which caused so much woe to those who benefited from her system, is a cause for rejoicing in heaven as the cry for justice uttered in 6:10 is finally answered (19:2b). The judgements of God may not be a popular subject, but 19:2 reminds us that with the right perspective they can be seen to be "true and just". The mention of the twenty-four elders and the four living creatures (19:4) tell us that we are back, once again, in the heavenly Throne Room of chapters 4 and 5. A voice from the throne itself (19:5) calls on all God's creatures to honour him – a reminder of 5:13 (cf Psa 148).

The wedding supper announced. 19:6-9

The fall of "Babylon" and the consequent establishment of the Kingdom of God (19:6b) is also the signal for the "wedding of the Lamb" to begin (19:6). The scriptural promises that the people of God are his bride (Isa 54:5; Jer 31:32; Eph 5:25-32, etc.) are about to be fulfilled. The bride has "made herself ready" by putting on the "fine linen" (i.e. the good works, 19:8b) she has been given to do (cf Eph 2:10). Nevertheless, it is not that we become Christ's by putting on good works, but rather that because we are his, we are *given* good works to put on.

• Compare Rev 19:9 with Matt 22:1-14.

• Who is invited to the wedding supper in Matt 22?
• Who is cast out?

The Message, not the Messenger 19:10

This section ends with an interesting cameo. John is tempted to honour the angel, rather as Cornelius was tempted to honour another messenger of God who issued an invitation to the marriage supper of the Lamb (Acts 10:25-26). We may contrast John's action here with his earlier response to the appearance of Jesus (1:17) where he "fell at his feet as though dead". There, Jesus placed his hand on John and spoke of himself (1:17-18). Here the angel tells John to stand up, saying that he is merely a "fellow servant" with all those, including John, who "hold the testimony of Jesus" – a phrase which has been used earlier to refer to ordinary Christians (6:9; 11:7; 12:11,17). It is the *message of Christ*, not the *messenger*, which counts in Christianity. These days there is a great tendency to look for new prophets and new visions as if we had exhausted all the prophecies and visions of the Bible and needed new insights! The lesson here is that *all* Christians who hold to "the testimony of Jesus" speak with "the spirit of prophecy". *All* Christians have something to say when they speak out the gospel. If they understand the Bible as well, and can explain and apply *its* prophecies, then they have a great message indeed.

Summary
Satan's greatest instrument in his warfare against the church is "Babylon". More people are deceived into unbelief by the world of comfort and luxury than by violence and oppression. "Babylon" is not the future 'kingdom of the Antichrist' but the Godless world system in any age. However, her destruction is assured both by the will of God and by the instrumentality of Satan himself.

▓ THE CONQUERING KING 19:11-21

The next two sections are the most difficult in the book in terms of relating what is described to historical circumstances. Interpretation hinges around the understanding of the so-called "millennium" – the thousand-year reign of Christ and the Saints (20:4,6) during which Satan is "bound" in the "pit" (20:2,3). Three views of this are given in the box below.

"And I saw" – the Victorious King and His Armies 19:11-16
The fact that John sees "heaven opened" marks this as another new section in the book (cf 4:1; 11:19; 15:5). This time he sees

VIEWS ON THE MILLENNIUM

Premillennialism – Christ returns before (pre-) the millennium

Christ returns with his saints, destroying the beast (usually identified with the Antichrist), the false prophet and all their armies. Satan is removed from the earth and 'bound' in the pit. Deceased Christians are resurrected to rule with Christ over the world. After a period of 1,000 years (the millennium), Satan is allowed out of the pit and leads a human rebellion against this rule. At the last moment, God intervenes and burns up the rebellious armies. Satan is thrown into the fiery lake where the beast and false prophet were thrown at Christ's previous return. All the dead are then resurrected for the final judgement. Death and hades are thrown into the lake of fire, as are unbelievers. A new heaven and a new earth are established.

Postmillennialism – Christ returns after (post-) the millennium

The church overcomes the powers of Satanically manipulated politics and false ideology (the beast and the false prophet) in the present age. Metaphorically, they are thrown into the lake of fire. There follows a period of peace and prosperity (the millennium) when Satan is 'bound'. His influence all-but disappears and the church can be said to rule the world. However, Satan's power is allowed to re-emerge for one great rebellion against God – the period of the Antichrist. This rebellion is defeated and Satan himself is thrown into the lake of fire as Christ returns to judge the world. Death and Hades are (metaphorically) thrown into the lake of fire, as are unbelievers. A new heaven and a new earth are established.

Amillennialism – the millennium is a metaphor for the present church age

In the present, the beast and the false prophet (the powers of Satanically manipulated politics and false ideology) oppress and oppose the church, but Satan himself is 'bound' in this period (the millennium). His powers are restricted and the nations are able to hear the gospel. From a heavenly point of view, Christians already live and reign with Christ. However, in the very last days Satan's power is released again on the earth, and a great period of deception and tribulation follows, including an unprecedented assault on the church – the period of the Antichrist. When Christ returns, with the Saints, he destroys these powers and all those who have followed them. Satan shares the fate of his followers. After this, the dead are raised and judged. Death and Hades are destroyed, and unbelievers go to their punishment. A new heaven and a new earth are established.

There are arguments for and against all these views. The best interpretation is likely to be the one which provides the 'best fit' to the Biblical material. The view we will take is that of 'amillennialism' (see also Appendix A), though some amillennialists would place less emphasis on the 'Antichrist' than we have done.

a rider on a white horse, clearly identified as Jesus by his name and appearance (cf 1:14; 3:14; John 1:1 etc.). But the fact that John does not simply say, "I saw Jesus", is a reminder to us that we are still in the realm of visions (cf the qualified statement in Ezek 1:28b). The blood on the figure's robe (19:13) is probably a reference to Christ's atoning death (cf 7:14) since it *precedes* his

treading the winepress of God's wrath (19:15, cf 14:17-20). Part
of the priest's role was to stand between the people and the wrath
of God (Num 18:1-5), and this was ultimately achieved by Christ
on the cross (Rom 5:9).

Riding with Jesus come the "armies of heaven" (19:14) who,
from their description, clearly include the church (cf 19:8)
though we would expect them also to include angels (cf Matt
25:31). The "sharp sword" which comes out of his mouth
(19:15, cf 1:16; 2:12,16) we know from elsewhere in Scripture
to be the word of God (Eph 6:17; Heb 4:12; Isa 49:2). 19:15
further indicates that the arrival of the armies of heaven marks the
fulfilment of the prophecies of Psalm 2 that the Messiah will rule
even the rebellious nations (cf 12:5; Phil 2:10).

Jesus has here three names: "a name inscribed which no one
knows but himself" (19:12, cf 2:17), "The Word of God"
(19:13, cf Jn 1:1), and "King of kings and Lord of lords"
(19:16). The title "King of kings" usually indicates worldly
sovereignty granted by God (cf Ezra 7:12; Dan 2:37), but "Lord of
lords" indicates divine status equal to God (cf Deut 10:17; Psa
136:3; Rev 17:14). Thus the Messianic King is both the agent
and the embodiment of God himself (cf Psa 45:6, KJV).

"And I saw" – the Supper of God's Judgement 19:17-18

The invitation of the birds to the "great supper" (cf Ezek 39:17-
20) contrasts with the invitation to the "marriage supper of the
Lamb" announced earlier (19:9). The latter symbolizes salvation,
the former, judgement. Included under this judgement are "all
men, both free and slave, both small and great" (19:18 cf. 6:15).
There is a reminder here that not all people who were poor or
mistreated in this life are automatically candidates for salvation.

"And I saw" – the Beast and his Armies Destroyed 19:19-21

The gathering for battle (19:19) picks up the earlier gathering at
Armageddon (16:16), but the battle is over almost before it is
begun. The "beast" of Satanically-manipulated political power (cf
13:1-10) is captured, as is "the false prophet", of Satanically-
manipulated ideologies (cf 13:11-17). *After this time Satan will neither
oppress nor lead astray either societies or individuals.* Both these enemies of
God are thrown into "the lake of fire that burns with brimstone"
(19:20). Clearly we are still in the realm of vision and metaphor here.

This is made even more obvious when "Death and Hades" are thrown into the same lake (20:14). We need not assume that there really is such a lake, much less that Death and Hades are 'things' which can be thrown into it. Yet the actual punishment of God's enemies will be no less terrible than this picture suggests.

The followers of the beast and the false prophet – all those who do not belong to Christ (cf 13:8) – are also destroyed by his word (19:21), just as the world was once *created* by a word (cf Gen 1). The feeding of the birds on their flesh (19:21) is followed in the similar passage in Ezekiel by the final in-gathering of God's people prior to the prophet's vision of the New Temple (Ezek 39:21-29). Thus we might assume ourselves to be reading here another account of the end of the world and the subsequent judgement (cf 6:12-17, etc.) to be followed by a passage describing the New Creation. But this description does not take place. The difficulty, however, is knowing where what *does* follow belongs in relation to what has just been described.

■ THE REIGNING SAINTS 20:1-21:8

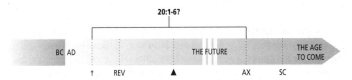

"And I saw" – Satan Bound for 1,000 Years 20:1-3

John now sees an angel bind Satan in the "bottomless pit" (20:1) for 1,000 years, during which time he is kept from deceiving the nations (20:3). This is clearly not his *final* judgement since at the end of that period he is released again "for a little while", only to be thrown into the lake of fire (20:10). However, past experience in Revelation should caution us against assuming that the events of 20:1-10 necessarily follow the events of 19:11-21 *chronologically*.

In order to locate these verses and the events they describe in relation to human history, we need to remember that the rest of Revelation seems to assume *one* great rebellion, not two, and similarly the rest of the Bible assumes a *second* Coming of Christ, but not a *third*. Moreover, there are significant similarities between the material in 17:7-14, 19:11-21 and 20:1-10, as we can see below.

17:8a The beast that you saw was, and is not...		20:2 [The angel] seized the dragon... and bound him for a thousand years, and threw him into the pit, and shut it and sealed it over him, that he should deceive the nations no more, till the thousand years were ended.
17:8b and is to ascend from the bottomless pit...		20:3 After that he must be loosed for a little while.
17:12-13 And the ten horns that you saw are ten kings who... are to receive authority as kings for one hour, together with the beast.	19:19a And I saw the beast and the kings of the earth with their armies...	20:7-8a And when the thousand years are ended, Satan will be loosed from his prison and will come out to deceive the nations...
17:14a they will make war on the Lamb...	19:19b gathered to make war against him who sits upon the horse and against his army.	20:8b to gather them for battle...
17:14b and the Lamb will conquer them, for he is Lord of lords and King of kings...	19:20-21 And the beast was captured, and with it the false prophet... These two were thrown alive into the lake of fire that burns with sulphur.	20:9b-10 but fire came down from heaven and consumed them, and the devil who had deceived them was thrown into the lake of fire and sulphur where the beast and the false prophet were, and they will be tormented day and night for ever and ever.

The events of 17:7-14 are paralleled by the events of 19:11-21 and 20:1-10. The same pattern is also found in a much abbreviated form in 16:12-16. *This suggests that all four passages describe the same event.* There is one great rebellion against God's rule, one great day of battle, and one return of the Lord Jesus to triumph over his enemies. The confining of Satan to the pit is therefore not something which takes place *after* a future return of Christ, but something which is effective now, and the 'millennium' is there-fore not a future event, but a present experience.

Supporting this conclusion is the fact that we have already had in 11:7 a reference to Satan coming up from "the bottomless pit" to attack the witnessing church. Similarly, the statement in 17:8 that Satan "is not, and is to ascend from the bottomless pit" seems to indicate his present confinement. In 2 Peter 2:4 God is described as having already sent the rebellious angels literally to 'Tartarus', defined in Strong's Concordance as "the deepest Abyss of Hades". In the Gospels, Jesus is the one who can bind "the strong man", meaning Satan (Matt 12:29; Mk 3:27; Lk 11:21- 22). The healing of the demoniac whom "no one could bind... even with a chain" (Mk 5:3) is both a striking confirmation of Jesus' power, and an interesting parallel to the angel's action in Rev 20:1! This same power over evil spirits is, of course, conferred on the disci-ples (Matt 10:1; Mk 6:7; Lk 10:19-20; Acts 8:7). There are also references in the Epistles, particularly in 2 Thess 2:3-8, which contains some striking parallels with the present section:

Let no one deceive you in any way; for that day will not come, unless the rebellion comes first, and the man of lawlessness is revealed, the son of perdition, who opposes and exalts himself against every so-called god or object of worship, so that he takes his seat in the temple of God, proclaiming himself to be God. Do you not remember that when I was still with you I told you this? And you know what is restraining him now so that he may be revealed in his time. For the mystery of lawlessness is already at work; only he who now restrains it will do so until he is out of the way. And then the lawless one will be revealed, and the Lord Jesus will slay him with the breath of his mouth and destroy him by his appearing and his coming.

Notice that Paul seems to assume the pattern we are suggesting – of Satan being restrained now, of one great rebellion, and of a deci-sive return of Christ to slay Satan "with the breath of his mouth" (cf Rev 19:15,21).

In what sense, however, is Satan 'bound' at present? He is still active in the world. His agents are still able to deceive many (1 Tim 4:1; 2 Jn 7). He attacks Christians (1 Pet 5:8), and can influence those who embrace his purposes (Jn 13:2). The answer would seem to be that, for the time being, he is limited to working through manipulation and instruments. He can manipulate human politics, so that the state becomes like the first beast, and can manipulate human ideologies so that false prophets arise. But his power is limited and the gospel is still proclaimed effectively. As John said elsewhere, "This is the *spirit* of antichrist, of which you heard that it was coming, and now it is in the world already" (1 Jn 4:3). But in the very last "hour" (17:12) Satan will be unbound and the Antichrist himself will be free to act.

"And I saw" – The Saints reign for 1,000 years, then Satan Released, Defeated and Destroyed 20:4-10

During this time when Satan is "bound" the Saints reign, but *they also are limited*. The mention of "thrones" and those seated on them (20:4a) takes us back once again to the heavenly Throne Room of chapters 4 and 5. The "souls" (20:4b) of those who had been slain as Christians had also been seen in the same context (cf 6:9). The RSV translation, "They came to life and reigned" (20:4c), is somewhat misleading, however. Literally the verse reads "*they lived* and they reigned with Christ". This condition of living and reigning with Christ is called "the first resurrection" (20:5), but we should note that they live only as "souls" and reign only for "a thousand years". Bearing in mind that 144,000 people need not represent the total number of the redeemed (cf 7:4,9), so also 1,000 years need not represent the total extent of this period. Instead, it could be a symbol of impregnability, like Hitler's boast of a "thousand-year Reich".

"Over such" participants in the "first resurrection", we are told that "the second death has no power" (20:6), but of course, by implication, the 'first death' (i.e. our ordinary mortality) *does*. Only at the 'second resurrection' will the power of this 'first death' be finally broken. Meanwhile, whilst that resurrection is still to come, the deceased saints dwell secure and share the reign of their already risen Lord.

The final rebellion by Satan forms part of that section of the vision which begins in 20:4. Whereas in 16:13 the deception of the nations is by Satan *and* the beast and the false prophet, here only Satan is mentioned (although we have argued it is the *same* rebellion). "Gog and Magog" (20:8) is the great enemy of Israel in Ezekiel 38-39. The rebellion is pictured as a march on God's city (20:9a, cf 11:1-2), but it ends as soon as it is begun (20:9b, cf 19:20), and the devil shares the fate of his agents in the lake of burning sulphur. (We may contrast this, of course, with the popular view of 'hell' as the place where Satan enjoys himself!) Thus, whereas 19:17-21 depicts the rebellion and defeat of the *human agents* of Satan, 20:7-10 depicts the defeat of their spiritual master – but, we would argue, it is the same rebellion and the same defeat.

"And I saw" – The White Throne of Judgement 20:11-15

The climax of the book of Revelation has come. The enemies of God have been destroyed, and the dead are about to be judged. Appropriately, therefore, John's vision returns to the one on the Throne (cf 4:2).

Whereas previously John had seen only the redeemed standing before the throne (6:9), now he sees all the dead "great and small" (20:12a, cf 19:18) who are judged on the basis of their deeds, written in the "books" (20:12c) which John sees opened. This judgement is both searching and inescapable – even the sea, Death and Hades give up their dead (20:13). Then Death and Hades, which have long been the terror of mankind, and whose power derives from the sin which is now being judged (cf Rom 5:12; 6:23), are themselves consigned to the fire (20:14). In this respect, there is indeed a joyous aspect to the final judgement! However, there is "another book" (20:12b) in which are written not deeds (by which we would all be condemned, cf Psa 143:2) but *names* (20:15, cf 3:5; 13:8; 17:8). Those whose names are in this book are saved from the second death (20:14-15), for it is "the book of life" (20:15, cf 21:27). Once more, the visionary nature of what John reports needs to be emphasised. We need not insist on there being literal books or a real lake of fire. Nevertheless, we may be sure that the reality behind the picture that John presents is no less terrible.

- What is the final basis of our judgement and our salvation?
- What should we be doing in the world as a result of this knowledge?
- What does it mean to call the lake of fire "the second death" (cf Matt 10:28)?

Summary

Though opinions may vary amongst Christians about the precise details, the certainty is that Christ will return in triumph and in judgement. He will destroy all his enemies, the living and the dead will be judged, and the reign of God will be brought in. The conviction expressed here is that Satan is presently bound, and that meanwhile the gospel may be freely and effectively preached to all nations.

"And I saw" – A new heaven and a new earth 21:1-8

Much of the imagery in this section is from Isa 65:17-25. Contrary to popular thinking amongst those who don't read it, the Bible is very reserved in its descriptions of the after-life. It neither menaces the sinner with lurid threats of Hell, nor seduces the saint with fantastic promises of heaven. The most compelling statement here is that "the dwelling of God is with men" (21:3). This has been the goal of redemption all along (cf Ex 25:8). We should note also the contrast between the popular view (even amongst Christians) that our ultimate destiny is to 'go to heaven' and the Biblical view which is that ultimately heaven comes to us.

The great picture at the end of Revelation is the re-uniting of heaven and earth, and the restoration of the original relationship between God and man which existed in the Garden of Eden (cf Gen 3:10). The passing of the old order means the undoing of God's curse on the world (21:4, cf Gen 3:14,17), and this restoration is total, encompassing heaven, earth and sea – the three great 'elements' of creation. (The comment that the sea was "no more" in 21:1 should not be taken as implying that there is 'no sea in heaven', but rather that this renewal of all things includes the sea, which has been an image of enmity and resistance to God in the past.) In this first glimpse, however, rather than describing the beauty of the new creation, John is first struck by the beauty of the new Jerusalem which is, in fact, the church (21:2, cf 19:7; 2 Cor 11:2). The inheritors of this new creation (the 'sons' of God) will be those Christians who endure to the end (21:7). But as the Garden of Eden was closed to sinful man (Gen 3:22-24), so the new creation is also closed to sinners (21:8a). The word here translated as "cowardly" is used twice elsewhere in the Bible referring to a 'lack of faith' (Matt 8:26; Mk 4:40). Unable to partake of what leads to life (cf Gen 3:22) there remains for them only the second death (21:8b).

- In the light of 20:6 and 20:14, what is the second resurrection?
- Why does the Bible say so little about the 'joys' of heaven?
- What is the chief joy of heaven described here, and why?

Chapter 4

The Final Act
Revelation 21:9-22:21

■ THE NEW JERUSALEM 21:9-22:5

"Come, I will show you the bride" 21:9-14

Even at this stage, John's vision has something left to reveal. In words paralleling the invitation to see Babylon (the 'anti-church' of 17:1) John is invited to see "the Bride, the wife of the Lamb" (21:9). He is again taken away "in the Spirit" (the subsequent description of the construction materials of the New Jerusalem will remind us this is a vision) and the beauty of the bride mentioned in 21:2 begins to be described in more detail (21:11-14). The six-fold repetition of the number twelve in this section (vv. 12,14,16,17,20,21) reminds us that the city itself is a symbol of the people of God, as do the names of the Old Testament tribes on its gates (21:12) and the New Testament Apostles on its foundations (21:14). There is more to the new creation, however, than the end of conflict or suffering. Rather, this is the beginning of the great and true marriage between the Redeemer and the Redeemed, of which human marriage is merely a symbol (cf Jer 31:32; Eph 5:30-32). It is the implications of this relationship, rather than its joys (which are unimaginable), which John goes on to describe in his closing verses.

The New Temple 21:15-22
As John once measured the embattled Sanctuary (11:1-2), so he is now told to measure the New Jerusalem. The city is a perfect

cube – each side being a multiple of twelve, as is the thickness of
the walls (21:15-17 – though it is crass to convert these measure-
ments into metres as does the GNB). Its nature as a Temple is
thus revealed, for the Holy of Holies was also a cube, though
much smaller (1 Ki 6:20) The description of the foundations is
also linked to Temple service, for as the priest's breastplate was
made of various precious stones bearing the names of the twelve
tribes of Israel (Ex 28:15-21), so the foundations of the city on
which the names of the twelve apostles are carved (21:14) are
also made of precious stones (21:19-20). The New Jerusalem is
thus perfectly equipped to be the new dwelling place of God with
his people (21:22, cf Ex 25:8). Formerly, the Temple symbolized
the presence of God in a segregated part of the city (cf 1 Ki 8:27-
29). Now, God is actually present and therefore is himself the
'Temple' in the whole of the city. We should also note that this
presence of God is the presence of "the Lord God the Almighty
and the Lamb" (21:22). You cannot have one without the other.

The Light of the World 21:23-27
Such a city has no need of 'lights', whether natural or artificial,
for it is itself the source of all light (21:23). Here, the concept of
"light" includes goodness, truth, understanding, righteousness
and so on (cf the use of light as a symbol in John 1:4-9 etc.). The
guidance – in Hebrew the torah – of God's "light" now extends to
all nations who come to him in homage (21:14, cf Psa 119:105;
Isa 60:3). And because it is the place of pure "light", and the
dwelling place only of God and his people, the city never needs to
shut its gates against danger (21:25-27).

The Life of the World 22:1-2
As the city is the source of the world's light, so it is also the source
of the world's life, for as a river flowed out of Eden to water the
world (Gen 2:10-14) so a river of life flows from this city (22:1-
2, cf Ezek 47:1-11) to bring life to the nations. The tree of life,
last encountered in the Garden of Eden (Gen 2:9b) is now seen to
be a whole orchard in the new Jerusalem (22:2b). And as was
promised to Abraham (Gen 12:3), the salvation (i.e. "healing")
of God is now extended to all the nations via the leaves of the tree
of life (cf Psa 67:2). The background passage in Ezekiel (Ezek
47:12) has the fruit for "food" (i.e. normal sustenance) and the

leaves for "healing" (i.e. the putting right of what is wrong), so that the forgiveness of sins is particularly in view here in Revelation.

The Servants of God 22:3-5
John recapitulates – there is no longer any curse (22:3, cf Gen 3:14,17). Instead the reigning God is present in the city (22:3). The RSV gives the action of God's servants as "worship" (22:3), but the word means "serve" and need not have a narrowly religious or 'cultic' sense. The picture is not of an eternal 'church service' but rather of the servants of the King carrying out his will. At last God is seen 'face to face' without threat (22:4, cf Gen 32:30; Psa 42:2). Moreover these servants themselves become co-rulers with God (22:5, cf Gen 1:26; Psa 8:5-8; Heb 2:5-9).

■ FINAL INSTRUCTIONS AND EXHORTATIONS 22:6-21

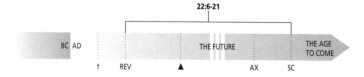

Yet even after all these visions, and our final glimpse of heaven, we must return to earth. Both John's first audience and we ourselves are actually living in the painful situations described earlier in the book. It may be some time before we reach either the first resurrection (20:4-6) or the second. The book closes, therefore, with renewed calls to *faith, endurance, patience* and *hope*.

The nature of this book as an *epistle* is emphasised by the rather fragmented nature of these final verses (cf 1 Cor 16:13-24; Col 4:16-18, etc). There does not appear to be a particular overall structure and therefore it is easiest to examine them verse by verse:

• 22:6 The truth of the book and its source are restated (cf 3:7; 1:1).

• 22:7 Believers are exhorted to act on what they have heard (cf 1:3) in the light of the imminence of Christ's return (cf 16:15). Our obedience to the word of God now is the guarantee that we shall be inheritors of life in that Day.

• 22:8-9 John testifies to his own witness to the message. His mention of the temptation to pay divine honour to the messenger may be a reminder rather than a repetition of what happened at the end of the revelation of Babylon (19:10 – the difference in wording is trivial and may be for clarification). Even if John actually repeats his mistake, the lesson is still to be faithful to the message and honour its source, rather than be overawed by the messenger. Blessings lie not in greater visions, but greater faithfulness to "the words of this book" (22:9).

• 22:10-11 Though the angel is the messenger, the message from here to 22:20a is from Jesus (cf 22:16). We are reminded that the message of the book is for now, not the future. It is not to be sealed up, but opened up (22:10). However, even with this book open to all, life will continue as normal – a mixture of sinners and saints (22:11).

• 22:12-16 Again there is a reminder of the imminence of the Lord's return (22:12a). The reward for endurance is on its way (22:12b). Jesus, the coming one, has the character of God himself (22:13, cf 1:8; 21:6). His blood has made possible entry to the New Jerusalem from which sinners will be excluded (22:14-15). It is also he who has sent the angel with the message (22:16, cf 1:1).

• 22:17 The proper response of the community of believers, wherein the Spirit now dwells and works (cf 1 Cor 3:16), is to long for and look forward to the coming of the bridegroom (22:17a). There is also encouragement for the unbeliever or the doubter to receive the free gift of life in the gospel (22:17b, cf 21:6).

• 22:18-19 The book closes with a warning. Its message is sufficiently important – and sufficiently terrifying - not to need any editorial 'help'. Nothing must be added to its message nor taken away from it (cf Deut 4:2). The same could usefully be said about the whole of Scripture!

• 22:20-21 Finally we are reminded that Jesus is, indeed, coming soon (22:20a). And together with John, we long for that day (22:20b). In the meantime, we live under his grace (22:21).

Summary
The final message of the book of Revelation is a call for *endurance*. As such, it is written for *every* Christian in *every* age. The experience of the Christian in the world is often one of hardship, persecution and perplexity (cf 2 Cor 4:8-12). However, our hopes are not set on this world, but on the age to come. "In the world you have tribulation; but be of good cheer, I HAVE OVERCOME THE WORLD" (John 16:33).

Conclusion
In conclusion, let us say this. If you are an unbeliever who has read Revelation, or if you are a Christian who has been disturbed by it, then notice again that 22:17 contains this encouragement: "let him who is thirsty come, let him who desires take the water of life without price". Comparing this with John 7:37-38, we see it is a call to believe in Jesus. The message of salvation is for whoever is thirsty, and until Christ returns the doorway to salvation stands open. If you would like to be sure that your name is in the book of life, and that you will not be excluded from the new Jerusalem, then come, "take the water of life without price".

Lord Jesus, I know that you are coming soon. I know that when you do, it will be to judge the world, and I know that on my own merits I cannot stand before you as my judge in that day. I recognize now that you died for my sins so that I could be made clean. I open my life to you and ask you to be my Lord and Saviour from this time on, even though serving you may bring persecution and make my life more difficult. Thank you for giving me new life and your Holy Spirit. Grant that I may endure to the end. Amen.

Appendices

■ APPENDIX A

More on the Millennium...
George Eldon Ladd, former Professor of Biblical Theology at Fuller
Seminary California, presents a scholarly argument for premillennialism in *The Gospel of the Kingdom* (Exeter: Paternoster Press, 1959).
However, on page 38 of this work he makes three crucial observations which reveal certain weaknesses in his thesis. First, regarding
Satan's rebellion following his binding at Christ's return and the
first resurrection, he admits that "One would never discover this
fact from most of the New Testament". Second, he notes that at
the end of the millennium "even though Christ has ruled over
men, Satan finds their unregenerate hearts still responsive to his
enticements and ready to rebel against God". Third, following
from this, he concludes "We might say, therefore, that the
Millennium *ends in failure* so far as the full achievement of God's
reign is concerned" (emphasis added).

Although Ladd's reputation is well-deserved and his presenta-
tion of his views is thorough, we feel that these observations reveal
a key weakness in millennialist thinking. Quite simply, millenni-
alism introduces more loose ends than it resolves. In particular, it
requires that the Second Coming of Christ and the resurrection of
the dead referred to in other parts of the New Testament is *not* the
end of this age and the beginning of the age to come. It also
requires us to accept that in a world where the resurrection of the
dead has taken place and Christ has reigned in person for a thousand years (and where presumably the Scriptures will be widely
available and fully understood so that books like this one will be
unnecessary) Satan will nevertheless be able to lead many people
into an inevitably unsuccessful rebellion foretold in the same
Scriptures which foretold Christ's return. Moreover, in this age
which begins with the first resurrection, there will still be death
since "Death and the grave are not destroyed until the final judgement at the end of the Millennium" (Ladd, p 38). But to whom
does this death apply? The resurrected Christians are presumably
immune, but what about believers alive at Christ's return (cf 1
Thess 4:15-17)? Or does death only apply to non-believers (surely
a bit of a 'give-away' as to whose side one should be on)?

The hardest suggestion to swallow, however, is that the Second
Coming to which Revelation so eagerly looks forward (22:17) will

end in failure. Ladd's difficulty is highlighted by the final paragraph in this chapter of his book (p 39):

> Furthermore, the Kingdom of God will never be fully realized apart from the personal, glorious, victorious Coming of Christ. [...] The powers of Satan and of evil can be finally overcome only by the mighty act of the return of Christ. But that day *is* coming! The Word of God urges us to watch, to be awake, to be ready for that Day. What assurance, what comfort, what stability it gives to our hearts and minds to know that our prayer will certainly be answered: "Thy kingdom come, thy will be done, on earth as it is in heaven." Yea, come quickly, Lord Jesus!

The irony of this paragraph seems entirely lost on Ladd, given his earlier admission that he believes the return of Christ will *not* in fact overcome the "powers of Satan and of evil". For our own part, however, we feel that in this paragraph Ladd's intellectual position is overcome by *Biblical* sentiments – and at *this* point we agree with every word he says!

... And a bit on the Rapture

Some readers will notice we have said nothing so far about the 'Rapture', nor have we suggested it as a possible solution to some of Ladd's difficulties. For those who have never heard of it, this doctrine teaches that before the period known as the 'Great Tribulation', true believers will be physically removed from the earth to be with Christ – resulting in such phenomena as driverless cars careering out of control, pilotless planes plunging from the skies, and empty pews in churches of the right sort the following Sunday. The world in the years immediately before the Second Coming will thus be entirely populated initially by unbelievers, though in most schemes new believers then have to emerge (usually convinced by the disappearance of Christian friends and the Bibles they leave lying around) in order to provide subjects for persecution. The reason for not mentioning all this is simply that I believe the doctrine of the Rapture to be totally mistaken. It seems to be based on a rather exotic reading of 2 Thess 4:17 first suggested by J N Darby in the nineteenth century. As with millennialist views, it is at variance with the plain reading of the rest of the New Testament and creates more problems than it solves.

■ APPENDIX B

Abbreviations of Bible books:

Gen	Genesis
Ex	Exodus
Lev	Leviticus
Num	Numbers
Deut	Deuteronomy
1 Ki	1 Kings
Psa	Psalms
Isa	Isaiah
Jer	Jeremiah
Ezek	Ezekiel
Dan	Daniel
Nah	Nahum
Hab	Habakkuk
Hag	Haggai
Zech	Zechariah
Matt	Matthew
Mk	Mark
Lk	Luke
Jn	John
Rom	Romans
1 Cor	1 Corinthians
2 Cor	2 Corinthians
Gal	Galatians
Eph	Ephesians
Phil	Philippians
Col	Colossians
1 Thess	1 Thessalonians
1 Tim	1 Timothy
Heb	Hebrews
Jas	James
1 Pet	1 Peter
1 Jn	1 John
2 Jn	2 John

NOTES

NOTES